Transforming Schools and Systems Using Assessment:
A Practical Guide

Second Edition

A Joint Publication

Transforming Schools and Systems Using Assessment:
A Practical Guide

Second Edition

Anne Davies, Ph.D.

Sandra Herbst

Beth Parrott Reynolds, Ph.D.

Foreword by Paul LeMahieu, Ph.D.

Published in the US by Solution Tree Press
555 North Morton Street
Bloomington, IN 47404

800.733.6786 (toll free) / 812.336.7700
FAX: 812.336.7790

email: info@solution-tree.com
solution-tree.com

Printed in the United States of America
15 14 13 12 11   1 2 3 4 5

Library of Congress Cataloging-in-Publication Data

Davies, Anne, 1955-
   Transforming schools and systems using assessment : a practical guide / Anne Davies, Sandra Herbst, Beth Parrott Reynolds. -- 2nd ed.
       p. cm.
   Rev. ed. of: Transforming barriers to assessment for learning : Courtenay, B.C. : Connections Pub., c2008.
   Includes bibliographical references and index.
   ISBN 978-1-935543-91-6 (perfect bound : alk. paper) -- ISBN 978-1-935543-92-3 (library edition : alk. paper) 1. Educational tests and measurements. 2. Educational leadership. 3. Learning. 4. Leadership. I. Herbst, Sandra, 1970- II. Reynolds, Beth Parrott, 1954- III. Davies, Anne, 1955- Transforming barriers to assessment for learning. IV. Title.
   LB3051.D3658 2011
   371.26--dc23
                        2011052494

Solution Tree
Jeffrey C. Jones, CEO
Edmund M. Ackerman, President

Solution Tree Press
President: Douglas M. Rife
Publisher: Robert D. Clouse
Vice President of Production: Gretchen Knapp
Managing Production Editor: Caroline Wise

Connections Publishing
Project Manager: Judith Hall-Patch
Editors: Annie Jack, Julie Watkins
Design & Layout: Beachwalker Studio, Ken Chong, Mackenzie Duncan, Kelly Giordano, Cori Jones

Contents

In dedication and deep appreciation:

Stewart, Bambi, Sheena, and Mackenzie Duncan

Edith and Steve Herbst

Mary and Wendell Parrott and Barry, Russell, Wendell David, and Keith Reynolds

Foreword

A wise friend once counseled that what we need to do to our education system for the sake of this and future generations of children is much too important to wait until we know exactly how to do it. His advice: "Fail fast and fail often." But how can this admonition be something other than a recipe for chaos? By seeing to it that there are commonly held goals and shared values. Then, as we stumble and pick ourselves up, our goals will ensure that we are facing the right way even as our values guide the path that we would choose.

This is a book about leadership, one of very, very many. It is a practical guide to the topic rooted in much experience and success, one of relatively few, indeed. It is also a book that concerns itself with the identification, adoption, and application of a set of values in and about leadership; this makes it just about the only book of its kind.

I have worked with teachers and professionals at all levels of education, and in my work, I find them increasingly reluctant to assume the mantle of leadership. At a time when genuinely enhanced capacities (including those for leadership) need to be distributed throughout and deeply embedded within all levels of the system, and at a time when we are recognizing (at last) the need for distributed leadership such that ideas can be interpreted, adopted, adapted, and ultimately implemented in wise, thoughtful, and constructive ways, educators' reluctance to accept the role of leader among peers is a disappointment that greatly diminishes the capacity of the system and its potential.

I find at least three primary causes for this reluctance. First is a culture of misplaced egalitarianism—one in which all must appear to be the same (reality notwithstanding) and, like the literal and metaphoric bucket of crabs, any that head off on their own are quickly pulled back. Second is an unfortunate and long-standing history of bad experiences with those who call themselves—and are ordained by the system as—leaders. Third, and one that would necessarily address the first two as well, is the absence of an acceptable alternative vision of leadership—one that is defined by its human values, yet practical in its guidance.

One vision of leadership that can profitably guide those in covenantal communities, such as those formed by teachers, school administrators, district personnel, and superintendents, or in other professional communities, is offered by Robert K. Greenleaf by way of Thomas Sergiovanni. It is a vision that has its roots in a story by Hermann Hesse, *Journey to the East.*

In this story, we see a band of pilgrims on a mythical journey. The central figure is Leo, a servant who does their menial work, but who also sustains the group with his spirit and song. He is a person of extraordinary presence, and all goes well for the pilgrims until Leo disappears. The group falls into disarray, and the journey is abandoned. They simply cannot make it without the servant Leo. The narrator of the story, after years of wandering, finds Leo and is taken into the Order that sponsored the journey. There he discovers that Leo, whom he had known first as a servant, is in fact the head of the Order. He is its guiding spirit and a great and noble leader.

This vision of leadership suggests that great leaders are servants first, and it is just this image of servant leadership that Robert K. Greenleaf offers us as an alternative to traditional views. In it, three things are required above all else: common goals, shared values, and an integrated communal presence. Motivated by a clear, consistent, and widely held view of where we are going and guided by humane values that suggest how it is that we want to treat each other and relate to the world around us, we are able to press toward the solution of problems and the accomplishment of great things. In this vision, the leader works alongside us, laboring with us, while serving as our monitor of goals and conscience of values. This provides the cohesion, the impetus, the sense of direction, and the common purpose necessary for groups to achieve. This is the form of leadership implicit in this book.

Contrast this view of problem solving to another that also relates leaders to their subordinates. Problems are solved in a manner that is repeated all too often. The Lone Ranger comes riding into town with his mask and mysterious identity. He never gets close to those whom he will help. His power is partly in his mystique. Very quickly, the Lone Ranger has understood the problem, identified the bad guys, and has set out and caught them.

And what do we learn from this hero? Among the lessons of this typical tale of problem solving are the following:

- There is always a problem to be solved by someone, and someone else is always responsible for doing so.

- Those who get themselves into some trouble are incapable of getting themselves out of it.

- In order to have the mystical power of leadership needed to solve such problems, the leader must stay behind the mask.

- Problems get solved by leaders, and everyone has every right to expect them to be solved quickly and decisively.

These myths are no laughing matter. Unfortunately, none of this bears any resemblance to the real world—not the one we live and work in and much less the one in which we would want to. The point here is the important place and nature of *responsibility* for each and every one of us, and in everything that we do. The myths also point out precisely why it is that we need to be guided by an alternative vision of leadership, one in which the role can be genuinely integrated into the work of the organization.

Subordinates do what they are supposed to do, and what they do is often shallow and perfunctory. Subordinates want marching orders. They want to be told what to do. *Followers*, on the other hand, choose to be led. They are self-directed. They work best without supervision, assessing what needs to be done, when and how, making any necessary decisions on their own. Followers are people committed to a purpose, a cause, a vision. Whatever they commit to, it must be a purpose that enriches themselves and others. *Followership* is a commitment to values and ideals. It is a responsibility to choose to follow (when appropriate) and by so choosing, to be a servant of ideals. Through that service one also becomes a leader.

This view allows genuine leadership to be situational, not just in its strategy, but also in its very presence and application. Each and any of us may, by occasion, be colleagues in a following role, or leaders as appropriate. At one moment or in one area, a leader, and in the next, a contributing professional colleague. And every one of us shares in the responsibility for the organization and its success. Only this organic view allows for the leadership and attendant responsibility to be distributed in ways that support success in modern organizations. It is the only form of leadership appropriate amongst communities of professional peers.

This is the vision of leadership implicit in this book, and we can all learn from it.

Paul LeMahieu, Ph.D.
The Carnegie Foundation for the Advancement of Teaching and
The University of Hawaii at Mānoa

Preface

"To cope with a challenging world, any entity must develop the capacity of shifting and changing—of developing new skills and attitudes; in short the capacity of learning."

Arie de Geus

The leader's journey will inevitably bring you to the river of learning. Some see this as a good time to quit. Others see an opportunity for a new and exciting experience, even knowing that there will be obstacles and tests ahead. Once you commit to the river, you can't go back; once you commit to change, forward movement is going to occur.

The only way to feel confident and reduce anxiety is to prepare for the ride, make a plan; choose a sturdy raft, a guide who knows the way, a committed team, and reliable equipment to keep you safe. Once you hit the rapids, bailing out doesn't work—you don't end up dry and safe onshore. Instead, abandoning the learning at this point leaves you going forward *without* your raft, your equipment, your team, and your guide.

As you enter and negotiate the rapids of system learning, let the successes of other leaders give you the courage you need to face the fear of the unknown. Then you will share the passion of meeting the challenge as a team and the exhilaration of surviving the "spin cycle."

Along the way, these rapids also have obstacles that need to be overcome. But we can't focus solely and pointedly on them. Rather, we need to concentrate on the water that flows between these obstacles, as it pushes and pulls us along our journey.

Getting from where you are to where you want to go requires continuous assessment *for* learning. It provides the processes leaders need to negotiate what lies before us and to plan next steps.

This book is jammed with examples of how you can lead the way to system change at all levels of education. Let the lessons learned by others support your preparation and implementation. You might choose to read it from front to back, or go directly to a chapter that focuses on a topic you are currently thinking about.

The journey requires that we pay attention to the following areas:

- Establishing a common starting point (chapter 2)

- Systemic focus and alignment (chapter 3)

- Time to reflect (chapter 4)

- Rethinking time and resources (chapter 5)

- Professional development that leads to learning (chapter 6)

- Expanding proof of success (chapter 7)

- Moving from resistance to support (chapter 8)

- Bridging the implementation dip (chapter 9)

- Involving parents and community (chapter 10)

- Increasing quality feedback (chapter 11)

- Standards-based reporting (chapter 12)

We have also included a task at the end of each chapter to get you started on practicing assessment *for* learning with your leadership team—your colleagues. We invite you to spend time considering these ideas in relation to any initiative. They work because all learning involves assessment *for* learning. That said, the examples in this book are focused on change in relation to classroom assessment and assessment for adult, school, and system learning. No matter what kind of learning you are seeking for yourself and your learning organization, assessment *for* learning will help you achieve your goals and stay on track to success.

This is not a step-by-step, how-to book—given the complexity of the work we do, we can't simply adopt previously used methods to suit the river that we need to navigate. However, the experiences of others help us find our way. As leaders, we need the research at our fingertips, so that when we are asked *why*, we are prepared to shine a light on validated research practices. We provide a collection of pertinent research summaries—brief descriptions of the key findings of those dedicated people upon whose shoulders we stand—that you can access in our companion resource, *Leading the Way to Assessment for Learning: A Practical Guide.*

Are you assessing *for* learning in your work as a leader? As you move forward, we ask that you adapt these ideas to your own context. To help you do that, we have provided a collection of templates, found as forms in the appendix, to assist you in your planning.

Assessment *for* learning helps inform our work by building bridges from problems to solutions. When we are heading downriver, we have to continuously assess where we are in relation to where we want to be, and what needs to be done in the moment. We seek continuous feedback. We watch. We consider what might happen next. We keep our focus. When we keep the end in mind, we use assessment *for* learning to keep ourselves on track.

Being a leader is always a work in progress and continually involves building relationships with others. Leaders know the work is never done—but what's important is moving towards success, purposefully and thoughtfully, while making a greater difference for more and more learners along the way. Assessment *for* learning is the process that makes great results possible.

This book, along with its companion, *Leading the Way to Assessment for Learning*, can help you to put into practice the principles and big ideas of assessment *for* learning. Whether your system is a school, a cluster of schools, or an entire district, we invite you to actively take on the role of learner—to not only use assessment *for* learning to inform your next actions, but to experience assessment *for* learning as the powerful learning structure that it is.

Assessment *for* School and System Learning: Leadership in Action

Contents

"To see the future, you have to travel on the rough edge of experience."

Harriet Rubin

Transforming education isn't about the latest great idea. It is about imagining the best possible future for our students and putting our hearts into our work, so we can take the next steps on the path. It is about building on the research and finding ways to make the seemingly impossible both possible and practical. Research has shown us that what we need to accomplish—deep student and organizational learning—isn't possible unless assessment *for* learning is the key focus of our work.

As leaders, our journey to success begins with the *end in mind* and uses assessment *for* learning to keep us on track and to provide tools for the journey. Assessment *for* learning propels systems toward success. Using the same steps that enable our students to achieve, leaders can employ assessment *for* learning techniques to plan for, implement, gather feedback about, and collect evidence of change for learning. This is an ongoing model of learning for the entire educational community. In education, the goal is organizational learning—constant, informed change.

Successful leaders don't attempt to do this work alone. System learning takes the wisdom of a crowd and the energy and passion of a leadership team devoted to helping each learner become all she or he can be by developing the skills, attitudes, and knowledge needed to learn and achieve success in life. As educators working together—respectfully, reflectively, and with great resilience—we can create ways to continually improve schools and learning.

Leadership Lessons

Like you, we are in positions of leadership, have read the books, have made our share of mistakes, and have learned from them. We've provided leadership both when it was our job and when it wasn't. Over time, we've learned some lessons and uncovered some truths that guide our work. Here are some of our guideposts:

Know yourself so your actions are aligned mindfully and thoughtfully. Reflection and self-knowledge are key. What matters to you? What lessons have you learned that might help others? Your responses to these questions are important preparation.

Plan and take action. Leaders begin with the end in mind. Do you know where you are going? Have you considered how you want to live your life along the way? Do you have the courage and patience to persevere? Do you remember the *big* destination you are working toward? Do you keep your eye on the next step? Do you know your goals and keep them in mind, minute by minute and day by day? Do you find ways to walk your talk? Reflect on your responses.

Plan for and consciously seek balance. As leaders, we must plan for balance so we can move forward with zest, foster resilience in ourselves and in others, make time to laugh and to celebrate, and encourage others to step back from the hard work and reflect. We do this in order to keep focused and engaged in the work to the end.

Walk the talk. It isn't good enough to say one thing and do another. As leaders, we need to be the change we want to see—including being a learner, a collaborative team member, a critical thinker, an effective communicator, and a good person. Acting with integrity—that is, being aligned in words and actions—is difficult but essential. We need to be mindful at all times, modeling focus and dedication in order to lead others.

Build and maintain relationships. Be respectful. Be polite. Be present. Involve and include everyone in the work. Invite others to shape and join the learning. Serve. Accept help. Receive gifts of time, assistance, resources, and feedback gracefully.

Reflect in order to learn. Give yourself the gift of critical feedback. What's working? What's not? Invite feedback from others. Learn from it. Use feedback to keep on track. Continuous quality assessment in relation to destination is key to understanding and moving forward towards your goals. The more complex the task of learning, the more assessment *for* learning needs to be thoughtfully employed.

Learn more. It is important that we be informed. Read the research. Consider the theory. Listen to your colleagues. Pay attention to what works.

Transform barriers. Pay attention to the things that get in your way. Know that each one informs the work; it is an opportunity to polish—to work with others to make the next steps even better. As leaders, we must plan strategically and take action, make sure we are focused on the right work, and use "second-order" change opportunities as defined by Marzano et al. (2005) to positively impact student learning through curriculum, assessment, and instruction initiatives. We must implement the plan and thus close the knowing/doing gap. Leaders transform challenges into opportunities, remaining open to better ideas and actively seeking solutions when the "tried and true" doesn't work.

The leaders in our lives—our families, friends, students, teachers, and colleagues—have provided us with *just-in-time* modeling.

Inside education, writers such as Phil Schlechty, Michael Fullan, Rick Stiggins, Paul LeMahieu, Robert Marzano, Douglas Reeves, Margaret Wheatley, and Andy Hargreaves have taught us that the center of our work must be children and their learning. Our success as a lead learner can only be determined by the success of all learners.

Outside education, writers such as Peter Senge, Tom Peters, Darby Checketts, and Malcolm Gladwell have taught us that leadership is intertwined with who we are and the context in which we work.

People in our world, such as Mother Teresa, Lance Armstrong, Stephen Lewis, Nelson Mandela, Paul Farmer, Severn Cullis-Suzuki, and Marc and Craig Kielburger have taught us that we can all make a difference by being leaders who nurture relationships and work together with others to make a difference. Our job is to decide where and what to do to help others.

Assessment and Learning Connections:

Terence Crooks researches and writes about educational assessment and the interrelationships among assessment, teaching, and learning. His 1988 summary of ten years of classroom assessment research, "The Impact of Classroom Evaluation Practices on Students," is a seminal resource for leaders seeking direct support for assessment *for* learning.

It seems that no matter how much we know or think we know, every initiative that involves learning and change (and they all do) will at some point cause us to flounder or stop in our tracks. But because children and their learning are at stake, we take the time and make the effort to reflect on the work. We reflect on our right actions and the best we could do given what we know and where we find ourselves. As educators, we know we are reinventing ourselves daily as we strive with more confidence towards a continually changing future.

Leadership in action requires new ways of meeting the challenges in today's schools. Historically, expectations of schooling varied for students with different levels of abilities. Now our job is to educate every learner so that each one graduates having met our prescribed high standards, as well as being prepared for a life of ongoing learning.

Assessment *for* Learning Impact Connections:

Assessment Reform Group—which includes researchers Paul Black, Dylan Wiliam, John Gardner, Wynne Harlen, and Gordon Stobart— has conducted meta-analyses focused on classroom assessment that guide assessment-related decisions.

What does it look like to be successful? Consider the lessons of books like *Talent Is Overrated* (Colvin 2008) and *Outliers* (Gladwell 2008), which speak to the importance of deliberate practice in order to be successful. These books and others also speak to the importance of recognizing that it takes more than good test scores to prove our successes. Today's standards are not so easily *measured*. Our success can only be *assessed* using a broad range of evidence collected over time. It is not enough to rely on assessment evidence generated by tests. Instead we are thoughtfully expanding the ways students can show what they know. Classroom assessment—both assessment *for* learning and assessment *of* learning—is needed to show proof that students have met the standards or learning outcomes.

Success results from continually assessing where we are in relation to where we want to be. Assessment *for* learning is the bridge between the first step and the last step on the path to success.

For learners, success comes from knowing what the learning destination is and what success looks like, being involved in setting criteria, self-assessing their way to success, and collecting evidence of learning. It is an informed partnership with teachers.

In the classroom, success involves individuals and groups of learners working together, using assessment *for* student learning to make learning and achievement possible for everyone.

For educators, it requires collaboration with colleagues in coming to agreement about what success in their role looks and sounds like, and in using assessment *for* adult learning to guide their way.

For an organization, success results from using assessment *for* system learning practices to become the optimum learning organization—one that begins with the end in mind and continually assesses its way to success.

For a family and community, defining success for themselves, as well as for learners and schools, can lead to improvement for all.

" *Managers are people who do things right, while leaders are people who do the right thing.* **"**

Warren Bennis

Consider the questions below, and select those that best fit your needs. They can be used to prompt a reflective conversation that engages your team in taking stock of where you are now in relation to assessment *for* learning in your district or school.

- Is this what we are meant to be doing?

- Where are we heading? Is this taking us where we need to go?

- Are we "walking the talk"?

- Are we reflecting on what's working and what's not?

- Is there a barrier we need to transform?

- Who do we need to involve? Who is missing?

- What feedback do we have and do we need?

- What evidence will prove we are heading in the right direction?

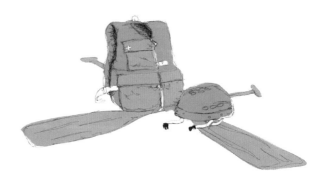

Establishing a Common Starting Point

Contents

" The greatest danger for most of us is not that our aim is too high and we miss it, but that it is too low and we reach it. "

Michelangelo

We are working to make a difference. We know assessment *for* learning will help us do a better job, but we are all in such different places with different ideas about what is needed. Leaders ask, "How do I make sure no one is left behind? How can we all move forward even though we have different starting points?"

When people in positions of leadership try to use assessment *for* learning to help all parts of the system learn, there may be people who share the vision and understand the end in mind, while others don't. As a result, there are gaps that can potentially become potholes or canyons, making the journey bumpy or simply impossible. Leaders, therefore, need to lead by example, explicitly applying the principles of assessment *for* learning. It also requires them to consciously and persistently involve everyone within the organization by deliberately linking the new work to earlier initiatives and by providing both support and pressure, thereby expanding the list of who is contributing to this important work.

We try to involve everyone from the beginning. We share our common vision for supporting all learners. We thoughtfully build diverse teams. We try to use consistent language. We reallocate resources—people, space, time, and money—to find creative ways to support the important work. We respect the diversity of ways people go about achieving the vision we all share. We appreciate and allow for multiple ways that people can show what they are learning—i.e., the evidence of their successes. We collect evidence of students' successes from multiple sources over time, looking for trends and patterns so we can learn continuously as we work.

When we are trying to get everyone going at the same time and in the same way, it is easy to leave someone behind. In our experience, the ones left behind are often the ones we assumed no one would forget. Take a moment now and make a few notes. Who are you leaving behind? Is it the support staff? The building principals? The high school teachers? The parents? The business community? The central office staff? The students?

Vision–Relationship Connections:

Tom Peters and Bob Waterman's leadership wisdom was first published in *In Search of Excellence* in 1982. Since then they have continued to encourage leaders to take action, to build relationships, and to acquire and grow the best employees. Their ideas have guided both business and education.

We've uncovered some simple yet powerful ideas that can ensure that everyone moves in the right direction. Here are some examples:

An elementary school connects parents who are new to the school community with those who have had children attending for a while, knowing that many questions are better explained parent to parent. A Frequently Asked Questions (FAQ) section in a parent handbook or on a website just isn't enough.

A secondary school provides every faculty member with business cards showing their name and contact information. The vision of the district, along with the website address, is printed on the back. When parents and community members speak to a faculty member, they are given a card so they can follow up if needed.

Community members attending the many school functions—sporting events, science nights, drama performances, and student exhibitions—are asked to provide specific feedback related to the learning goals of the event. This feedback is shared with students, school faculty, and the district office.

A superintendent's organization produces "talking points" on a variety of topics related to school system initiatives. When they are asked to speak to different community groups, these talking points are used. Retired superintendents volunteer to be kept informed and are asked to help out with speaking engagements when needed. This organization also places notices in newspapers and on bulletin boards that provide information about different aspects of education in today's world.

A middle school faculty, as part of its outreach, invites community members to participate in student showcase conferences. Students collect evidence of their learning over time and present their evidence at a conference that includes not only their parents and faculty members, but also community members. Everyone is encouraged to ask questions and give feedback.

Periodically, faculty members from across a school district gather to listen to students from previous years talk about what helped them learn and what got in their way. This experience helps everyone remember that they can learn from both successes and failures. Their success as an educational community is reflected in every one of their students—and especially in those who struggle to learn.

One school district, knowing that school and district-based office staff respond to many questions from parents and community members, involved all support staff in key professional development opportunities, along with certified educational staff. When role-alike learning groups were formed, they discussed ways to implement the ideas in their context. After hearing a presentation about beginning with the end in mind and setting criteria with students, one elementary school secretary decided to set criteria with the group of sixth-grade students who answer the phones while she is on break. This allowed her to improve the quality of the service students provided to people calling the school, while supporting the classroom learning goals.

Overall Message—Involving students in their assessment increases achievement levels.

Top Three Talking Points	Visual Representation
- Students need to know what the standard is so that they know where they are headed - Refer to Black and Wiliam research - When students know what quality work looks like, they will see what they need to change in their work. There are no surprises.	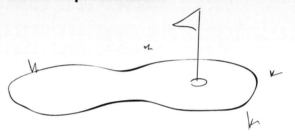

Possible Audiences	Possible Methods	Possible Opportunities
- Board of Trustees - Parent councils - Parents	- Presentations by students at a board of trustees meeting - Brief articles in school newsletters	- parent-teacher conferences - free community newspaper

The Communication Planning Tool outline can be found as a reproducible on page 144 of appendix 2.

An elementary school prepares each student from 4 to 13 years of age to present on a topic related to the school's learning focus. At some point in the year, parents and community members are invited to come and listen to the students in each grade present what they have been learning.

A school principal takes groups of students, groups of staff members, and groups of parents and community members out for an inexpensive lunch and invites them to talk about what is working and what could be improved.

Dissonance–Discovery Connections:

Jerome Bruner viewed cognitive dissonance as the key to learning. This is where discovery involves a reorganization of one's existing *truth* in order to account for new ideas. For further reading, see *The Process of Education, Toward a Theory of Instruction,* and *The Culture of Education.*

" *True vision is far-reaching. It goes beyond what one individual can accomplish. And if it has real value, it does more than just include others; it adds value to them.* "

John Maxwell

 Lessons Learned

- Listen and seek to understand before seeking to be understood. Know the difference between dialogue and discussion. Structure a variety of ways to get input and feedback from a range of people and perspectives.

- Consider metaphors, symbols, and graphics to help people understand key ideas.

- Establish feedback loops. Routines and rituals that form a web of persistent communication and dialogue are necessary and require ongoing care. Be conscious of increasing the number, kind, and speed of the feedback loops you build, since the more variety you provide, the more responses are likely. The figure on the facing page documents feedback associated with a student-led conference initiative.

- Involve everyone. Make a list and check it twice. Then check it again. Keep a watch for who is being missed. Add to your list regularly. Find ways to invite new perspectives into the conversation, including the voices of the dissenters.

- In relation to the shared vision of success, develop a shared understanding of the evidence of success along the way—both small and large steps towards success. Use this list to identify and celebrate successes early and often.

- Say it briefly, often, and in different ways. It is essential that leaders represent key ideas mindfully and simply, in a variety of ways over time. See page 12 for a sample Communication Planning Tool.

- Model continuously. Leaders must find ways to model the work they are asking of others.

Moving forward together means acknowledging where people are and where they need to be, and finding ways to help them close the gap. Feedback that feeds forward to learning is one way we use assessment *for* learning to keep everyone on track and close the gap.

Initiatives: Student-Led Conferences (Tsolum School)			
Individual or Group	Opportunity for Feedback	Feedback Received	Feed Forward Planning & Action Taken
Parents	Anon. Survey	93% responded. Incredibly positive suggestions about offering parent-teacher conferences if needed as well as suggestions for parents with more than one child.	Ask parents of more than one child if they want their conferences scheduled back-to-back. Ensure teachers let parents know they can request a parent-teacher conference if needed after the s-p-t conference.
	Focus Groups (held two sessions)	23 parents in attendance.	Advice to self: Make sure students are comfortable participating. Action: more practice needed.
	Attendees at conference filled out surveys	97% responded. Most positive. Helpful suggestions. See additional notes.	Advice to self: Publish agenda ahead of time. Try to help parents be better prepared.
	Principal's Office Open Door: Parents invited to stop by office to provide feedback	Lots of compliments Complaints: conferences running late; some parents who want to meet with teachers alone and didn't realize they could sign up. Suggestions: more evening conference times for working parents.	Action: Meet with classroom teachers to discuss ways to meet more parents' needs regarding scheduling. Look for a win-win solution or combination of solutions.

Assessment–Motivation Connections:

Martin Covington's research and writing have been largely focused on understanding the motivational dynamics of school achievement. His findings on learners' avoidance of public failure by disengaging from learning or choosing less demanding work challenge educators to reflect and re-examine academic goals and prevailing reward structure.

Task for the Leadership Team

Consider the message that you need others to hear, and complete the template of the Communication Planning Tool on page 144 of appendix 2. A sample outline is found on page 12.

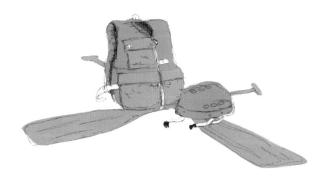

Systemic Focus and Alignment

Chapter 3

" Few, if any, forces in human affairs are as powerful as shared vision."

Peter Senge

Contents

We know assessment *for* learning is important and positively impacts student learning and achievement. But there are so many initiatives competing for our time and attention. How can we select and maintain a focus on assessment *for* learning in a way that serves a larger purpose? And how do we align system priorities, policies, and practices so they don't get in the way of the work to be done in assessment *for* learning?

As leaders, our role is to lead others. Part of this important work is to recognize that focusing means consciously choosing and making connections among the actions that will yield the highest results in student and system achievement and learning. We must all do this in an informed, systemic way. Our work is to choose actions that embed and sustain assessment *for* learning.

Alignment Connections:

Thomas J. Sergiovanni is an internationally recognized author of educational leadership. His work has helped schools and systems rethink how they can operate successfully. His five dimensions of leadership—technical, human, educational, cultural, and symbolic—are lenses through which effective leadership practices can be strengthened.

As teachers redesign their classroom structures and practices to better reflect the *big ideas* of assessment *for* learning, so school districts need to reconsider and align their practices, policies, protocols, and procedures with these same ideas. To expect only classroom teachers to shift in their work in the absence of systemic realignment is to separate the interdependent parts of the whole.

To begin, apply, and model the lessons of systems thinking, help others see the work both close up and from a system's perspective. In Marcel Proust's words, "The real voyage of discovery consists not in seeking new landscapes but in having new eyes." Standing back allows us to make better sense of why and how the work serves a purpose beyond our own. It provides a lens through which to interact, choose strategies and actions, and move forward collectively. Understanding from a system's view will allow everyone to prioritize and carefully focus, so energy and resources are well spent.

Systemic Learning Connections:

Peter Senge writes about innovative learning organizations in terms of systems thinking, personal mastery, mental models, building shared vision, and team learning. From an assessment perspective, his work is particularly important because of the reliance on continuous reflective feedback.

As we move forward, we need to embed assessment *for* learning into the culture and conversations of our schools and support systems. In other words, leaders must also consider broader structures and regulations that enable the work. How can we transform the flood of tasks into a single, manageable, tightly focused stream of energy? We develop systems and procedures to support the use of a full range of data (qualitative and quantitative) to inform professional judgments of staff across the system. We choose high leverage actions and strategies that align with our desired results. We take into account both summative and formative assessment.

Much of what we know about the power of systemic focus and alignment of policies, protocols, practices, and procedures comes to us through the eyes and ears of others who have thoughtfully applied its lessons. A few examples follow:

One school district selected assessment *for* learning and change as the focus for five years. Visuals depicting the linkage of the two were crafted and widely communicated. Professional learning days were focused on assessment *for* learning. School personnel were assigned to cohorts for ongoing and job-embedded learning. During this shared experience, participants actively constructed knowledge within team learning time and then assumed responsibility for sharing with others. Additionally, individual departments within schools determined an aligned focus for collaborative work that supported the larger purpose of the district. They scheduled times for sharing their proof of learning and for jointly determining next steps.

A superintendent, along with representative principals and central office leaders, synthesized and visually framed connections between assessment *for* learning, standards-based design, instructional strategies, and professional learning. The visual representation was used to communicate the assessment *for* learning initiative to a diverse range of audiences, helping them see the district vision in a unified way, regardless of which leader was sharing information about the initiative.

To jump-start the learning and build a common language and understanding of the vision, the district attended first to the learning needs of leaders. Agendas for monthly cabinet (superintendent and key leaders from each department), principal, assistant principal, and instructional coach meetings were reframed to focus tightly upon what standards-based classrooms look like when implementing assessment *for* learning. Guiding questions and selected proof statements served as the organizers for monthly conversations.

A superintendent asked the question, "Where do we want to be in five years?" All school departments collaborated in justifying requests and goals in terms of their impact on their agreed-upon purpose: advancing student learning and achievement through assessment *for* learning. These back-and-forth discussions helped sharpen the focus and caused individual departments to reconsider their requests in light of collective needs. Group decisions regarding those needs determined to be "not urgent" were collaboratively determined with leadership teams' guidance.

A large urban school division reviewed its procedures to hire new administrators and used the triangulation of evidence as its frame. Interested candidates were invited to submit a résumé, a statement of educational leadership, and an outline of their experience (product). The ensuing interview process (conversation) also involved in-basket activities that asked people to respond, in writing, to a contentious article and to triage a list of tasks, while describing their thinking of the order in which they would address the issues (product). Superintendents spent one half-day observing the candidates in their work and role in the schools or district (observation), followed by a meeting with the candidates' immediate supervisor (conversation). The candidates also participated in a mock interview with a person acting as a journalist. This was videotaped and viewed (observation) by the superintendent's department. The process allowed the leaders of the school district to gather evidence over a longer period of time, under different circumstances, and across a variety of situations. In their deliberations, the superintendents were able to note trends and patterns in behavior and make decisions based on reliable data.

A district's teacher evaluation procedure was rewritten to include triangulation of evidence. In the past, summative teacher reports had been framed from the sole perspective of the principal, after a few classroom observations. Now, teacher products (student work samples, lessons, and unit plans), teacher self-assessments, data from focused classroom observations, and conversations with parents, students, and the teacher himself are required to construct a thorough, rigorous, reliable, and robust report.

A district's grading protocol was redesigned to limit the percentage mark or grade on report cards to achievement data only. Consideration of attitude, effort, participation, and homework completion was reported to parents in a different section of the report card, through the use of a three-point scale and anecdotal comments.

A high school staff reconsidered its position of posting students' marks or grades daily or weekly based on that day's work. Students now have the time to learn, collect feedback, engage in reflection and self-assessment, and readjust their thinking, understanding, and work before a mark or grade is given and shared with parents.

A district's assessment policy was revised and reframed in a way that is conceptual rather than procedural. Guidelines outline principles that balance assessment *for* learning with assessment *of* learning. The policy's big ideas value the role of student, teacher, and parent, while considering the importance of assessment as an ongoing and natural part of teaching and learning.

A curriculum coordinator of a large urban school district recognized that though assessment *for* learning had been a focus of professional development for two years, there had been little impact on classroom practice. Through conversation, teachers indicated that the structure and expectations of the traditional report card did not align with their deeper understanding of assessment and evaluation. In considering this feedback, the district re-examined its vision in curriculum, instruction, and assessment, and as a result, worked with teachers to develop new report cards based on curriculum standards/outcomes. (The report card samples on the following page illustrate two of the choices.)

River East Transcona School Division Policy—IKA

(excerpts)

The board of trustees recognizes that assessment promotes student, parent, teacher, and system learning. Its role and purpose can be divided into assessment *for* learning and assessment *of* learning.

Assessment *for* learning is the process of seeking and interpreting evidence for use by learners and their teachers to decide where the learners are in their learning, where they need to go, and how best to get there.

Assessment *of* learning is a summary of information collected about learning in order to share that information with others.

Assessment in schools is to be undertaken in accordance with the following principles:

- Assessment supports and reflects curricular outcomes.
- Assessment engages students.
- Assessment focuses on "what" and "how" students learn.
- Assessment recognizes all educational achievement.
- Assessment is part of effective learning and teaching.
- Assessment involves students, parents, and teachers working collaboratively.
- Assessment is an ongoing, systematic process.
- Assessment is balanced and multifaceted.
- Assessment respects the dignity and reflects the developmental needs of the learning.
- Assessment is equitable and fair.
- Assessment is a key professional skill.

Thanks to River East Transcona School Division, Winnipeg, MB.

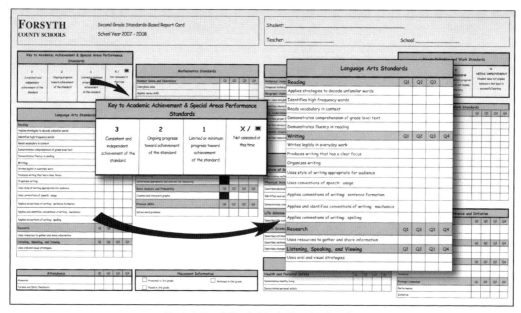

Thanks to Forsyth County Schools, Cumming, Georgia.

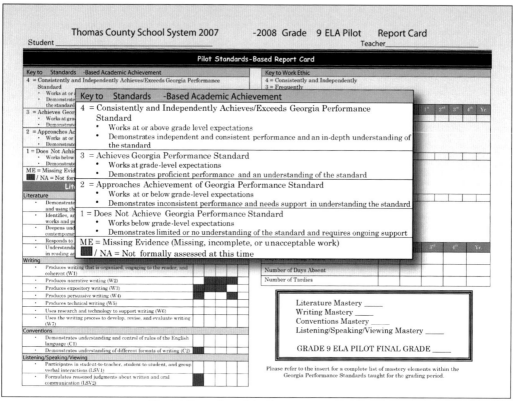

Thanks to Thomas County School System, Thomasville, GA.

A middle school re-examined its practice of end-of-unit testing and determined that it failed to honor multiple sources of evidence. Students now are asked to show what they know in a variety of ways, including oral reports, performance tasks, and student-teacher conferences.

A middle school replaced end-of-year exams with exit interviews. As part of this new reporting procedure, students prepare answers to four essential questions that encompass the year's learning standards/outcomes. They present their reflections to a panel that includes teachers, an administrator, a fellow student, a district representative, and a parent. They also use evidence of their learning to demonstrate their understanding.

" If you don't know where you're going, how are you gonna know when you get there? "

Yogi Berra

Lessons Learned

- Recognize that establishing and widely communicating tight priorities gives everyone permission to allocate time and resources selectively. The end result is a sharper focus upon what matters most. This gives others the freedom and encouragement to abandon actions that are not leading to success and take time for actions that better contribute to the agreed-upon purpose.

- Communicate, collaborate, and seek consistency. Change of this magnitude—second-order change—requires careful planning for and monitoring of these three Cs. Once priorities have been established, collaboratively determining and communicating roles and responsibilities is essential so that all players understand their role in the larger purpose. When used mindfully, routines and rituals form a web of persistent communication and dialogue.

- Frame and communicate the end in mind visually. A simple,

graphic depiction of where we are headed provides a clear goalpost for learners at all levels, thereby building critical mass as we collectively inch closer to desired results. (See sample on page 28.)

- Give up what doesn't work. Tom Peters (2005) reminds us to keep a Don't Do list. This list is as valuable as To Do lists since we need to identify those things that are not as important or act as a barrier to the work we are meant to do.

- Heed lessons from reputable research. Research has provided us with a clearer picture of what works and what does not work in schools. Use research to provide the "warrant," the "why," or the imperative of the focus, priority, or strategy.

- Close the knowing and doing gap. Stop planning and start doing. Bob Eaker writes, ". . . it is important to understand that a learning community is not created by completing a series of tasks but rather by beginning a process of perpetual renewal. This process calls on each member of the faculty to regard the continual search for better ways of fulfilling the school's mission and responding to change as integral parts of their daily responsibilities" (DuFour and Eaker 1998, p. 284).

- Identify a process to review district practices, policies, protocols, and procedures at all levels. Do they support, detract from, or interfere with your focus on assessment *for* learning?

  o Examine the historical context that brought about the practice, policy, protocol, or procedure in relation to the required change. Determine whether the practice, policy, protocol, or procedure should or can change. Is it connected to an external directive or requirement?

  o Be clear with your staff when a practice, policy, protocol, or procedure cannot be changed. Publicly share the reasons why and provide a strategy for staff to reframe, cope, or work with the practice, policy, protocol, or procedure.

  o Decide whether, as a leader, you will change or alter the practice, policy, protocol, or procedure by:

    • Making the revisions entirely by yourself

    • Seeking input, but still making the final decision

    • Collaborating and cooperating with others to create a new practice, policy, protocol, or procedure o Create a representative team to lead the change if a collaborative model is optimal. Build in a series of feedback loops to constituent groups (administrators, teachers, trustees) and hold focus group conversations. Build in a review of current research to not only inform the revision, but to support the leadership team's learning. Identify a communication, implementation, and learning plan around the new practice, policy, protocol, or procedure, as required.

Process of Policy Development (Sample)

The Program and Policy Committee of the Board of Trustees formed a committee of teachers, administrators, district-level personnel, and an assistant superintendent.

The committee met several times over the course of a year and a half to:
- Learn about and review research related to assessment
- Review current policy
- Collect and review policies from other school districts
- Decide whether the policy framework would be a procedural or a conceptual one
- Identify principles of assessment and indicators for each principle
- Draft a policy
- Establish a plan for feedback and revision, including a frame to organize the feedback

A presentation of the draft policy was made to the three administrative councils (early, middle, and senior), and feedback was gathered using the frame.

The committee reviewed feedback, and changes were made.

A teacher representative from each of the 42 schools participated in a focus session, and feedback was gathered using the frame.

The committee reviewed feedback, and changes were made.

The revised document was again presented to the level administrative councils and to a second teacher focus group.

The committee reviewed feedback, and changes were made.

An external consultant was engaged to review the draft, meet with the committee, and suggest changes.

The committee reviewed feedback, and changes were made.

The Program and Policy Committee of the Board of Trustees reviewed the final draft document and also provided feedback.

The committee reviewed feedback, and changes were made.

The final document was presented and recommended to the entire Board of Trustees by the Program and Policy Committee of the Board of Trustees and was formally passed into policy.

It is important to note:

- Not all changes that were suggested were made. The committee compared the feedback to the research around assessment and made changes in an informed fashion, using consensus building as a model.

- Feedback sessions with the Board of Trustees, administrators, and teachers always included time for learning about assessment.

- Members of the committee facilitated feedback sessions so that there would be an understanding of the context of the sessions in which to consider the feedback.

- The working committee made suggestions to the Superintendent's Department regarding policy implementation and communication plans.

Thanks to River East Transcona School Division, Winnipeg, MB.

- Be prepared to demonstrate how you, as a leader and as a member of a leadership team, walk the talk along with the classroom practitioners. Remember that alignment builds confidence, commitment, ownership, and buy-in.

- System change requires the work and the engagement of the entire system. It does not occur when only one part of the system (i.e., teachers) engages in assessment *for* learning practice.

Systemic focus is a powerful quality control tool. Assessment *for* learning across the system gives us a vantage point from which we can reflect and influence learning in the best possible way. By deliberately choosing what efforts, evidence, and strategies we will implement in relation to our end in mind, we greatly increase the likelihood that we will, in fact, reach those goals and be able to trust the ultimate results.

Systemic Learning Connections:

Michael Fullan, an internationally recognized authority on education reform, is engaged in training, consulting, and evaluating system-level change projects. He has written extensively about managing and driving educational change, focusing on building leadership capacity, supporting effective change, and promoting deep learning.

However, systemic focus requires that we pay attention to alignment of policies, practices, protocols, and procedures. It signals to others what the organization holds as important and models the use of assessment *for* learning to inform practice, protocol, procedure, and policy. Our challenge is not to be so tightly aligned that there is little opportunity to be responsive to emergent issues and needs. It is in striking this balance between alignment and flexibility so that leaders can impact increased student learning and achievement.

Using the Review Checklist below, review your district's assessment policy and the degree to which it reflects assessment *for* learning principles.

Review Checklist

The policy reflects these principles of assessment *for* learning . . .	Met	On the Way	Beginning	Not Yet Met
Supports and reflects curricular outcomes and standards	✓			
Engages students in the learning process as partners	✓			
Focuses on "what" and "how" students learn		✓		
Recognizes all educational achievement, not just academic	✓			
Honors assessment as an ongoing, systematic process	✓			
Involves parents		✓		
Requires assessment to be balanced and multifaceted	✓			
Respects the dignity and reflects the developmental needs of the learner		✓		
Is equitable and fair		✓		
Recognizes assessment as a key professional skill	✓			

An outline of this figure can be found as a reproducible on page 145 of appendix 2.

Considering the example provided below and others from your own experience, develop a visual representation of the systems that are connected to assessment *for* learning initiatives for your district or school.

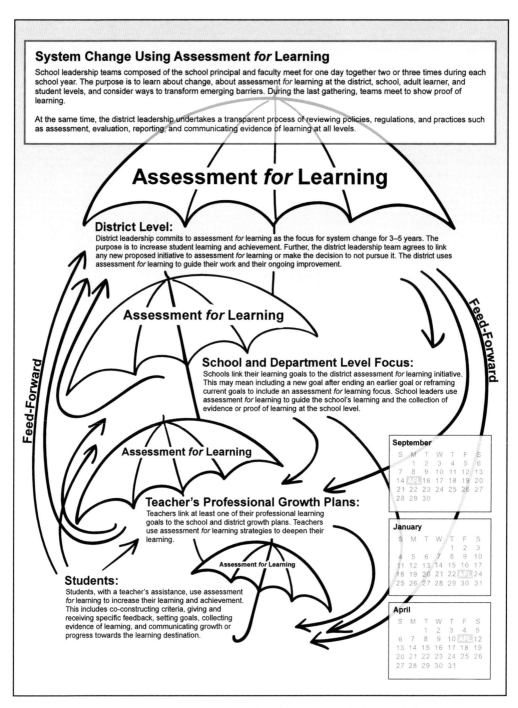

This figure can be found as a reproducible on page 146 of appendix 2.

Time to Reflect

"To read without reflecting is like eating without digesting."

Edmund Burke

Contents

Reflection is the pause between action and reaction; the more we pause and reflect, the better the quality of our actions. We are in such a hurry. Our time is limited. Yet, learning depends on reflection. How can reflection become a valued part of our work? If we aren't walking the talk by modeling appropriate assessment practices and using assessment *for* learning to reflect and keep ourselves on track, how can we possibly expect everyone else to do so? How can we build in assessment *for* our own learning so that we can truly be learning communities within a learning organization?

As leaders of learners consider the impact of assessment *for* learning on student achievement, it is important that all those involved in the change consciously and deliberately pause to engage in reflection. Without reflection, change becomes very difficult to manage. Some think we don't have time to reflect. Others may even say we don't need to reflect. After all, we are able to articulate the district's vision. We work as a member of multilayered teams. We collect evidence of the system's and of students' progress over time. We build and use common language. We creatively reallocate resources. We don't have time to reflect. Yet, without reflection time, there can be no learning.

Between communicating via text messages, emails, and telephone calls; attending meetings; writing memos; spending time in classrooms; talking with teachers; observing students; taking part in exhibitions; communicating with parents, community leaders, and boards; mentoring; dealing with controversial issues; reading; interpreting policies; and planning, it seems that there is little time or energy left to reflect. Teachers' days are also full. They are busy teaching; collecting lunch money; doing recess duty; planning class lessons; organizing the next school assembly; communicating with parents, grandparents, administration, and district specialists; working as part of a team;

searching for information about a challenging topic; interpreting standards/outcomes; engaging in professional reading; providing feedback; involving students in developing and using criteria; and much, much more.

When we are caught up in the day-to-day routine, it is also easy to neglect opportunities for reflection, especially since some of us assume that it is a luxury we can ill afford and others wonder what purpose it serves. Talking about the importance of reflection is not enough. We must value the practice of reflection, and consciously and purposefully identify time and structures for reflecting.

Here are some simple yet powerful ideas used to incorporate reflection into a busy schedule:

> A districtwide leadership team includes in its agenda a time for reflection at the end of each meeting. Individuals contribute to the group's learning by reflecting on the meeting and how it meets the committee's mandate.

> A middle school principal builds time into monthly faculty meetings for staff to individually reflect on progress toward their personal professional growth plans. Their reflections, along with evidence (may be an example, an anecdote, or in product form) are then shared in small groups.

> A district superintendent's department framed its weekly meetings around a structure of For Learning, For Information, and For Discussion. The For Learning section included an article, research report, video clip, or book chapter that focused on the district's stated priority of increased student achievement through assessment *for* learning. After considering how to implement the new information, time was set aside for reflection, allowing this team to refine activities and directions based on new understandings.

> The English department in a secondary school engaged in an action research project about expository writing. At department meetings, staff exchanged pieces of student writing and assessed them, using criteria that had been created with the students. They looked for trends and patterns across these samples in order to identify next steps for focus lessons. At the end of each meeting, teachers

reflected on the changes in student writing that they were noting over time, to determine the effectiveness of their direct teaching.

A school district ran yearly peer coaching training sessions. Staff members were invited to attend the seminar that spread across eight days during the school year. The goal of the sessions was to build participants' capacity to guide reflective interactions and to support others' self-directed learning. Skills of paraphrasing and questioning provided a structure to help colleagues think about their experiences, explore refinements, and construct new learning.

Coaching Connections:

Art Costa and Robert Garmston developed *cognitive coaching* in 1984. They define it as a set of strategies and a way of thinking and working that support self-managing, self-monitoring, and self-modifying. The goals of cognitive coaching include establishing and maintaining trust, facilitating *mutual learning*, and enhancing growth toward *holonomy*. (See figure on page 34.)

A district staff development person offered a series of after-school mathematics "power hours." He included time to write in a personal journal at each session. The entries encouraged participants to reflect on the products and processes of the session and to consider applications for their classroom practice. (See figure on page 32.)

A first-year elementary teacher kept a professional portfolio that chronicled her students' progress. These work samples allowed her to see student achievement over time. Written personal reflections by the teacher that focused on her teaching strengths and needs were included. This later became part of the evidence she chose to use as part of the teacher evaluation process.

A university professor included a blog for student communication as part of his online course design. Students from different jurisdictions wrote about their progress towards the course requirements and reflected on their experiences in a virtual classroom. The professor used those comments to plan next steps.

A high school teacher shared reflections of her own learning from student work and invited students to consider the growth of their work and thinking over time. She prompted their reflection for future learning by describing her next steps.

❝_An event is not an experience until you reflect upon it._**❞**

Michael Fullan

Reflecting Frame	
Recollection	I observed a class of grade 9 students assessing their work against a set of criteria that they had set prior to beginning their science inquiry. Students used the criteria to highlight for themselves where in the draft product there was evidence of each element. They shared their evidence with a classmate. Next steps will include time for revision to include missing elements.
Application	As I think about this classroom example of using criteria, I am reminded that it could be a powerful tool in connection with our department head meetings. We have identified six norms of collaboration but have not spent the time to describe them more carefully. Each of those norms could mean something different to each individual.
Insight	The common understanding that this detail brings could strengthen group reflection at the end of meetings. We could also share our criteria with our students to serve as a model and teaching tool. We should not expect our students to self-assess if we ourselves are not prepared to do so.

An outline of this figure can be found as a reproducible on page 147 of appendix 2.

- Value reflection. Describe the purpose and benefits of practicing it. Provide evidence that past reflections were considered in subsequent planning cycles. Do not judge others' reflections; they will be less likely to make their thinking public in the future. Consider saying "Thank you" and refraining from any further comment.

- Model reflection. As a leader, take the opportunity in front of your staff to make your thinking public. Reflect on how you came to make a decision. Talk about a challenge you face and how you are working through it.

- Provide structure for reflection. Offer frames, sentence starters, or conversation templates that allow staff to practice and focus on the skill of reflection. (See figure below.)

- Structure reflection into all professional learning. Purposefully build time into agendas for participants to shine their "flashlight" both forwards and backwards.

- View reflection as essential to goal setting. Thinking about the current state and comparing it to a goal or desired state identifies a gap that can become the next step.

Reflection Stems

I feel good about . . .

I used to . . . but now I . . .

My goal is . . . I will know I am on my way when . . .

One thing that worked today was . . .

One question I have . . .

Two things I will remember are . . .

If I could do something again differently, I would . . .

- Build time to reflect between actions. Stepping back from a situation may be all that is required to reconsider what happens next.

- Consider reflection as self-feedback. Construct new knowledge as you turn the feedback cycle inward.

- Establish a cycle for the larger system to reflect. Provide opportunities for constituent groups to pause and think about system activities and evidence that has been collected.

- Reflect with others. Identify a critical or listening friend from inside or outside the organization. Learning is amplified when done in groups.

The Reflecting Conversation

Summarize impressions and recall supporting information and data
- What do you recall about the experience/action?
- How do you feel about what happened?

Analyze causal factors
- Why do you think that _____ happened?
- What seems most important to consider/remember?
- What are some of the patterns/trends that are emerging?
- How is this experience similar/different to _____?
- What might be some of the values/beliefs/assumptions reflected by what happened?
- What kind of help might have been useful to you?
- How might you account for what happened?
- How does this compare to previous instances?
- What did you think would happen?
- How does this compare to what you already know about _____?
- What did this experience remind you of?
- What do you think was going on for _____?

Construct new learnings
- What connections/implications will be helpful into the future? Why?
- What will be important to remember for the future? Why?
- What new learning are you taking from this experience?
- In what ways can this experience be helpful to you?
- What might you do differently next time?

Adapted from *Cognitive Coaching* by A. Costa and B. Garmston. www.cognitivecoaching.com

- Adopt a stance of inquiry. Ask questions that are divergent in nature, rather than closed.

- Talk about the importance of reflection as a validated practice. In the same way that it increases student achievement, it supports teacher effectiveness.

- Establish learning communities that consciously build trust and rapport. Sharing personal thoughts with others can only happen in a genuine environment.

Learning communities are places for people to learn and grow. This occurs with reflection. It is in looking backwards that we can feed energy, ideas, and innovation forwards. Reflection is a key cornerstone in assessment *for* learning.

Reflection Connections:

John Dewey defined reflective thought as "active, persistent, and careful consideration of any belief or supposed form of knowledge in the light of the grounds that support it and the further conclusions to which it tends" (Dewey 1910, p. 6).

Using the questions in The Reflecting Conversation on page 34, reflect on a recent experience that relates to your work in assessment *for* learning. For example, you might choose to reflect on a workshop or seminar that you facilitated or participated in, a meeting that you chaired, a conversation that you had with a colleague, or an article that you read.

Then, using the Reflecting Frame outline provided on page 147 of appendix 2, record the recollections, applications, and insights that resulted from your reflections. Refer to the sample on page 32 of this chapter.

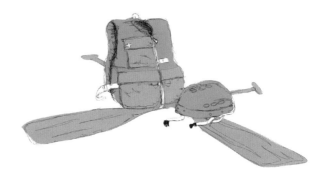

Rethinking Time and Resources

"There are incalculable resources in the human spirit, once it has been set free."

Hubert H. Humphrey

All learners need to engage in assessment *for* learning continually, whether as an individual learner, a professional learning community, or the learning organization itself. How can we find the time and resources to do all this?

The demand for more time, money, space, and people is a common theme that school leaders hear. Teachers cry out that they need more time to collaboratively plan lessons and to share examples of student work with each other. Grade-level teachers suddenly discover that the resource materials that they have do not match the new learning goals for their students. Teachers and principals realize that in some cases the expertise needed to coach students and to involve them in the assessment *for* learning process does not exist within their building or their district. Staff developers search for focused and job-embedded professional training around the new work of assessment *for* learning. Superintendents recognize that current organizational structures and staffing patterns in their districts may not match the vision. Current budgets and daily schedules have very little wiggle room. The school system realizes the need for different technology applications and for revised policies and procedures to support and allow for increased levels of collaboration, shared conversations, feedback, reflection, and goal setting—and wonders where it will find the time and resources. Accountability demands compel us to work smarter, not harder, and dictate some forced choices in terms of allocation of resources.

Yet we also know schools and districts that move ahead in spite of seemingly insurmountable constraints. What lessons can be learned that may have relevance for us in our journey? Often the solution is not found to be simply having more resources. Great schools and districts are willing to reinvent themselves to achieve the agreed-upon results. They are willing to reallocate and refocus resources and time creatively and flexibly when they see that they support their collective vision.

Rethinking time and resources means:

- Reflecting upon the existing infrastructure and the degree to which it supports the desired outcomes

- Using and modeling assessment *for* learning principles in framing and having conversations with groups

- Dedicating resources and time for deep learning

- Assessing what is working and what is not

- Matching human and capital strengths to needs and next steps

- Sacrificing individual preferences for the collective good of the organization

- Doing things differently

- Thinking outside the box in ways that are flexible, innovative, and creative

Professional Learning Connections:

Bruce Wellman and Robert Garmston write about characteristics of professional learning that overcome the challenges of time, getting work done, and doing the right work. Their work in adaptive schools provides school staff with resources and strategies to create collaborative norms, to design and conduct effective meetings, to engage in learning-focused conversations, and to become skilled at group facilitation.

Many simple yet powerful ideas for fostering innovation and refocusing and reallocating resources have emerged from schools and organizations to guide this work. Here are some examples:

One school district extended flexibility to individual school principals and to departments within the school district to use personnel allotments differently; in one such case, several principals opted to restructure assistant principal slots to create instructional coach positions dedicated to teacher support and job-embedded learning.

An assistant superintendent calmed anxious principals and assistant principals with the catchphrase: "How do you eat an elephant? One bite at a time." Over the next three years, it served as an effective benchmark and encouraged celebration of significant milestones along the way. The motto was also a good reminder that change is not an event, but a process.

A superintendent required annual budgeting requests to be presented in an open forum with all departments present. Each department was asked to justify to the group how their request would support the long-term goals and agreed-upon results for the district. The discussions caused many individual departments to reconsider their resource requests in light of collective long- and short-term needs that the group decided were more urgent.

Superintendents from several school districts joined together and pooled resources to create a professional learning series on assessment *for* learning. They hired a consultant to help them plan and lead the sessions. Every school in these districts participated, sending a team made up of a principal and five or six teachers. After actively taking part in the annual event, each team presented a portfolio of evidence of their learning to their colleagues and detailed next year's goals and possible evidence.

A superintendent won approval from the school board to refocus and reframe the job descriptions of some of the technology support personnel to become instructional technology specialists for teachers rather than computer problem solvers. In support of assessment *for* learning in classrooms, teachers and students were assisted in using technology to enhance learning, produce evidence, and keep track of progress. Emerging classroom needs became a financial priority for future technology budgets.

A district surveyed teachers to ask them to self-report on how well they had implemented several of the assessment *for* learning strategies. Teachers who indicated that they were at a level to teach others were invited to share their expertise and examples with colleagues in small learning groups.

One large urban school district developed a process to support principals in screening the myriad of professional learning requests flowing across their desks. The end result was the creation of criteria aligned to the district's major growth priorities. Principals were then asked by the professional learning director to use the criteria list to guide them in approving future professional learning requests.

A rapidly growing district determined that it would never reach critical mass without developing experts within. Principals were asked to recommend teacher leaders for training in assessment *for* learning. These teacher leaders were given release time to involve students in the assessment process and to develop a common framework for sharing their learning with others. Subsequently, they were called upon to lead small learning communities of their peers throughout the school year.

Teacher Leadership Connections:

Roland Barth is the founding director of Harvard University's Principals' Center and the author of several books. His work centers around educational reform and school culture. He asserts that leaders need to be active learners and they must create a culture of rich teacher leadership that values and celebrates the craft knowledge of the practitioner.

Many schools and districts have devised creative and context-appropriate strategies to carve out time for learning together. A number of these strategies are identified in the book *Finding Time for Professional Learning*, edited by Valerie von Frank (2007) and published by Learning Forward.

The teaching and learning division in a large school district decided to reallocate money spent on external conferences to support focused learning of leaders within all schools in the district. Agendas for monthly principal and assistant principal meetings were reframed to focus tightly on agreed-upon learning topics and next steps. Time was allocated for shared learning, and the monthly conversations were based on guiding questions.

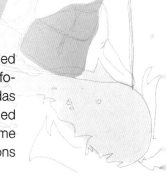

Ideas for Transforming Time

Criteria	Brainstormed List of Ideas
Keep Focused and On Track	• Focus on what matters most. • Less is better. Go for quality not quantity (explain to parents and others). • Address change as a schoolwide system. Put effective support systems in place. • Integration—look for ways to serve more than one goal at a time. • Spend the time up front and save time later. • Simplify so everyone understands and can use less time to do the task. • Manage stress levels. Keep a Don't Do List. Workload—drop off lesser priorities. • Use teacher and leader strengths to encourage and allow thinking and risk-taking. • Get feed-forward information to improve over time. • Deliberately improve and increase professional knowledge to work smarter. • Collect and show evidence. Be prepared to do less with greater depth. • Make AFL part of the culture and embed the work. • Chip away. Focus resources purposefully.
Set Goals and Persist	• Prioritize—make it important. Minimize interruptions. • Slow everything down and zoom in. • Set priorities/realistic (achievable) goals for school and staff. • Small steps—make one change then acknowledge that change. • Set goals and collect evidence of change over time. • Little steps—move forward persistently. • Use professional growth plans to give time.
Take Time to Teach and Give Time to Learn	• Teach process of feedback—skills of feedback, peer assess—to speed learning. • Help each other with time management. • Share understandings. Purposefully regroup children and adults for learning. • Share positive feedback from leaders. Value steps towards learning. • Provide incentives (time?) to engage in observation and peer feedback. • Focus professional learning time. • Involve more people. Ask everyone how can time be reshaped? • T.I.M.E—slow down to the speed of learning. • Reduce internal interruptions. Reinvent staff meetings. Creative time allocation—think smarter. Use ground rules to be efficient. • Delegate—get everyone involved so more people learn. • Mentor and coach day-by-day and bit-by-bit. • Use time table to support the work. Adapt timetable. • Hold breakfast and dinner meetings with release time to be used when wanted. • Provide learning time and needed resources to save time. • Professional development/learning can save time. • Provide time to be leaders. Bring coaches into the classroom. • Acquire/create professional development for leaders. • Create opportunities for dialogue (e.g., combine classes for short periods/try block scheduling/try different school calendars). Release during day. • Let go of guilt. Bring learning into classrooms. Learn every day. • Accept there will be different rates of learning—teachers, students, leaders, parents.
Listen and Seek to Understand All Perspectives	• Remove resistance to change—e.g., highlight benefits to children. • Work towards creating a culture that values collaboration and best practices. • Create opportunities for dialogue. • Invite resistant people to take a leadership role. • Set individual rates of learning/acceptance by staff. • Make it manageable. Set realistic and achievable expectations. • Educate teachers, students, parents, B.O.T. about importance of AFL. • Involve trustees, parents, and community members as part of study groups.

Notes from the Hawke's Bay and Wanganui seminars, New Zealand and Vancouver Island seminars, Canada (2006–2007).

The leadership team in an elementary school changed its school start and end times (adding 10 minutes to the instructional day) to accumulate minutes that they could reallocate to staff learning.

In another elementary school, *a learning day* was held every six weeks. It was a time when all teachers had their turn to meet together for focused staff development. While teachers from two grade levels met for their 90-minute sessions, their students joined other classes in cross-grade instructional activities. Parents and support staff assisted with the groups.

A school district convinced the school board and the community to allow the district to dismiss schools early six times a year so that teachers and principals could learn together. Three of the six afternoons were devoted to common school-based learning and work, organized and led by the principals and faculty leaders; the other three afternoons were devoted to across-district professional learning conversations and work around agreed-upon topics.

Another school district allocated professional learning dollars to fund special projects related to their vision. This included six days of substitutes, so that forty K–12 teachers could meet and work together throughout the year on developing standards-based report cards.

"It's not that I'm so smart—it's just that I stay with problems longer."

Albert Einstein

Lessons Learned

- Pool resources with neighboring schools and districts, sharing professional learning opportunities. In this way, leaders can save money, illuminate common strengths and concerns among teachers, and foster collaboration and team building. Feedback from teachers and principals participating in multi-district professional learning experiences always confirms the value of collaboration and conversation with other educators. Through this broader exchange, teachers share strengths, weaknesses, and struggles with other districts and often gain new ideas and possible solutions.

- Strengthen professional learning by sending teams or pairs to learning opportunities—not individuals.

- Increase *real* meeting time by handling informative faculty and district leadership meetings through email and/or memo.

- Identify potential experts within your system and dedicate time, energy, and money to developing them. Relying exclusively on external experts is costly and ineffective in terms of building internal capacity. A plan for developing experts within all levels of the organization will increase its competency as well as the efficacy of its members.

- Allocate resources based on long-term plans as well as short-term actions. Both are important to maintain forward momentum.

- Develop structures for monitoring results and for shared decision making. Solicit ideas for creative and flexible ways to apply resources and time from those who are charged with making it work.

- Collect data, administer surveys, and provide feedback and updates about the impact of resource and time uses. This ongoing feedback/feed-forward to learning and doing helps an organization improve.

- Decide what you are going to stop doing in order to have the time to do something new.

- Mindfully consider the Train the Trainer model of professional development and whether it will actually provide needed support. Often, people with limited experience cannot *redeliver* powerful and essential messages to their colleagues but can lead powerful conversations and replicate and share activities.

To truly be learners and demonstrate our commitment to assessment *for* learning and continuous improvement, we must make wise use of people's gifts, time, and resources. Effective leaders build an infrastructure for taking action, and foster innovation and flexibility in all parts of the organization for the people who work within it. They mindfully allocate resources in ways that enable and mobilize leadership to do purposeful work.

Task for the Leadership Team

Tom Peters challenges us to keep and continually add to a "Don't Do" list (see below). Accept this challenge and take some time right now to figure out what can go on your own "Don't Do" list.

Don't Do List

- Don't stay after 5:30 p.m.

- Don't eat while standing up.

- Don't have an open-door policy all day long.

- Don't respond to angry phone messages too quickly.

- Don't send long emails.

- Don't forget to delegate.

With thanks to Tom Peters.

An outline of this figure can be found as a reproducible on page 148 of appendix 2.

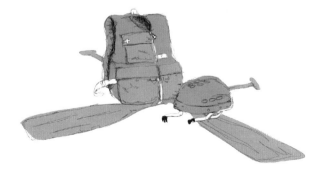

Professional Development That Leads to Learning

> *"Professional renewal is an essential ingredient in good teaching that we neither buy nor have bestowed upon us; we renew ourselves by revising who we are and what we do, daily and consciously, alone and together with students, colleagues and friends."*
>
> *Lorri Neilsen*

We know professional learning is needed, but how can we know what works and how to keep it working? How can professional learning be structured to make a difference?

The best professional learning experiences are not one-size-fits-all. When we pay attention to what learners know, what they need to know, and their preferred ways to engage and construct their own learning, we model good teaching practice and build professional learning experiences that work for everyone. As leaders, we *must* use assessment *for* learning to keep professional development plans on track. We check for continuous feedback, because as every good teacher knows, the important part of learning is whether the concepts and ideas have been understood, applied, and articulated.

Research has clearly shown that assessment *for* learning supports increased student achievement. All educators need a deep understanding of how this process works, but many are at different places along the learning continuum. Teachers need to engage in deep learning to more fully understand assessment *for* learning so that new practices can be established. School districts know better than to assume that a shift in classroom practice will occur after a single workshop and one-dimensional professional learning opportunities. Conceptual understanding requires multiple opportunities to do the work with feedback.

There are many models that can frame professional learning. One of these models (Champion 2004) reflects the need to offer opportunities at several "levels"—initiation, skill development, implementation, and institutionalization. The first level raises awareness; the second level encourages trial and practice; the third level focuses on making adjustments and refinements; and the last level focuses on maintaining these behaviors and strategies.

The learning opportunities in any professional development plan also need to reflect the characteristics of adult learning design—learning styles vary in adults just as in young students. Adult learners also benefit from:

- Being engaged

- Having choices

- Being supported to take risks

- Being involved in assessment for their own learning

Our experiences remind us that professional learning for educators is founded on inquiry and collaboration (Darling-Hammond et al. 2009; James et al. 2007; Schön 1983). Therefore, robust professional development encourages teachers to learn together by expanding knowledge, and by examining, questioning, and developing assessment practices. Much of what we learn comes through talking with others and being able to control our own learning process. We must engage learners in collaboratively constructing knowledge. Without the opportunity for participation, we will not move the learner from surface awareness to deep understanding.

The principles of assessment *for* learning—knowing what you want or need to learn, identifying what you already know, and developing the path to close that gap—support this active construction of knowledge.

Effective professional development must respect different entry points, strengths, needs, and preferences. Learning opportunities need to be multiyear, multilayered, and differentiated, and to include an evaluation plan. Here are some examples:

A school district developed a professional development plan around the three phases of learning—*activate* (year one), *acquire* (year two), and *apply* (year three)—by a leadership team of teachers, administrators, and district-level personnel. This plan signaled to all staff that though there were district expectations about the implementation of an assessment *for* learning policy, changes need not occur overnight. Rather, the plan reassured staff that there was time to learn, reflect, and practice; support would be provided. Each year's focus became increasingly more intense; learning moved from overview sessions to smaller learning teams engaged in action research, book studies, and classroom visitations.

A school administrator had teachers identify their own professional growth plans to change beliefs, attitudes, and practices regarding assessment. Teachers assumed the primary responsibility and accountability for their professional growth by identifying individualized goals and learning strategies. Some teachers chose to engage a peer tutor, others formed a study group, and others chose to take a college course on assessment *for* learning. In these ways, the learning was job-embedded and unique to their own needs and styles. School-based professional development funds were available to teachers to work toward goals. There was an expectation and support provided for teachers to share their progress, experiences, and results with others in the school community. Time for this purpose was scheduled at faculty meetings. Teachers also met with the principal or assistant principal throughout the year to consult and review their plans. (See sample on page 48).

Teacher: Susan Smith, Grade 4
Area of Focus: Expository Writing
Connection to School Plan: Improve Student Writing

STEP ONE

ACTION AREA	WHAT AM I GOING TO DO?	WHAT PROFESSIONAL SUPPORT IS REQUIRED?	WHAT DOES THE BASELINE STUDENT EVIDENCE TELL ME?
Specify current level of student performance.	• Identify curricular standards that speak to expository writing. • Set criteria that describe quality expository writing. • Assess samples of students' current writing against criteria.	• Read *Setting and Using Criteria*. • Read *Six Traits of Writing*. • Engage teaching partner with whom to talk through samples.	• Simple mechanics of writing are attended to. • Complex mechanics of writing are not consistently applied. • Few personal connections are present in the text. • Author voice is not strong. • Writing is organized around an introduction, body, and conclusion. • Students can focus on the topic. • Writing needs to be extended to include more detail.

STEP TWO

ACTION AREA	WHAT AM I GOING TO DO?	WHAT PROFESSIONAL SUPPORT IS REQUIRED?	WHAT DOES THE STUDENT EVIDENCE TELL ME?
Create an action plan: • Specify a measurable, instructional goal. • Describe teaching practice. • Describe assessment practice with time lines.	By the end of the semester, • Students will write three expository pieces that meet the criteria that will be set jointly with me and the students. • Provide samples of expository writing. • Use samples to develop criteria. • Model expository writing. • Read expository texts to students.	• Teacher colleagues review criteria that have been set in class. • Read chapters/articles about expository text. • Teach a lesson with a valued colleague.	

STEP THREE

ACTION AREA	WHAT AM I GOING TO DO?	WHAT PROFESSIONAL SUPPORT IS REQUIRED?	WHAT DOES THE STUDENT EVIDENCE TELL ME?
Evaluate progress.			

An outline of this figure can be found as a reproducible on page 149 of appendix 2.

A family of schools identified assessment as a common area of focus. While research in the area of assessment asks us to examine the balance between assessment *of* and *for* learning, professional development plans also need to consider a balance between required learning and invitational opportunities. A professional development plan with elements of both was created. The plan included meetings and sessions that all staff had to attend. However, choices were also offered in order to meet individual learning needs. For example, a book study was initiated for those interested in reading a particular text. Others opted to join a "Dine and Discuss" series that explored short passages and articles over dinner. Still others decided to observe lessons, followed by a debriefing protocol. When staff came together during the mandatory sessions, structure and time were provided for teachers to make connections and to share the learning from their diverse experiences.

Professional Learning Connections:

Etienne Wenger and Jean Lave coined the term *community of practice*. A growing number of people and organizations, including educators such as Richard DuFour, identify communities of practice as a key to supporting learning and improving performance.

A school district brought in an external consultant at strategic points throughout the implementation of a multiyear professional development plan. An initial session with all district staff provided a shared experience that both motivated staff and contextualized future action and learning. Recognizing the importance of providing learning opportunities to the people and groups who are leading the learning, the consultant worked with the district assessment leadership team to support and enhance learning. At a later date, school-based assessment leadership teams, groups of teachers, school staffs, and families of schools met together under the consultant's guidance. This not only supported the work that was being done internally, but pushed the staff to the next level of their learning. The external expertise both complemented and strengthened capacity for internal leaders and learners.

A district chose to link a districtwide focus on increasing the engagement of high school students and assessment *for* learning. One of the deliberate changes they made was to change titles, moving from Department Heads to Learning Coordinators. The shift in language was accompanied by changing job descriptions towards a focus on instructional leadership as part of the school leadership team.

The superintendent of one rural school district identified three teachers (one each at elementary, middle, and senior high) whose practice embodied the concepts and strategies of assessment *for* learning. They received training in peer coaching and facilitating groups. They then spent half of their time working in other schools and classrooms, providing "just in time" support to teachers who were revising their own assessment practices. These teacher-coaches modeled strategies with students, helped to plan clusters of lessons, and supported the professional growth of their colleagues.

A district leadership team created a survey to support planning after identifying assessment *for* learning as a focus for system-wide professional development. All K–12 staff completed a self-assessment that dealt with the hallmarks of assessment *for* learning: i.e., setting and using criteria, identifying for students the learning destination, involving students in self-assessment, and reflecting and goal setting. Teachers considered whether they *had met*, *had not yet met*, or *were working towards* the hallmark and were expected to include statements of evidence of their practice. This structure consciously modeled a process of reflection that teachers could adapt for use with their students. Administrators met with the teachers to review their self-assessments. Findings were compiled at the school level and submitted to the district. A district assessment leadership team analyzed the results of the self-assessments and a plan to address areas of need was created. In this way, the plan was framed not on hunches, but through the use of trends in data. The results of the survey and the professional learning plan that resulted were published and distributed throughout the system.

Feedback–Learning Connections:

Donald Schön's early work focused on learning systems within organizations and communities. He was one of the first thinkers to conceptualize learning organizations where "feedback loops" inform the system and guide learning.

A district assessment committee used the concept of triangulation to evaluate the impact of its professional development plan. *Products*, such as lesson plans, student work, and test scores, were collected over the course of two years. School plan outcomes and result statements were examined. Teachers engaged in self-assessment (conversations) that allowed them to reflect on their past practice and the manner in which it had shifted over time. School administrators reported on their observations of assessment *for* learning practices at the classroom level. District-level personnel collated these sources of evidence, and the findings were then compared against the district outcomes that had been identified. Summative statements were published to the broad learning community and included statements to indicate which elements of assessment *for* learning were being used in classrooms, the level of teacher understanding of assessment *for* learning principles, and the level of student engagement in the assessment process. The information was used to determine strengths, areas of need, and next steps.

A district professional development committee investigated the various professional learning structures beyond the single workshop. Their collated list included:

- Grade/department meetings
- Action research
- Conferences
- College/university courses
- Book studies
- Study groups

- Data analysis

- Lesson study

- Lesson observation

- Mentoring

- Peer coaching

- Teacher portfolios

- Case studies

- Live or video models

- Interviews/audio conferences

- Self-directed study

- Dine and Discuss

- Conversation protocols

- 30-minute meetings

- Team teaching

- Collaborative planning

- Individual professional growth plan

- Professional reading

- Blogging

- Emailing an expert

- Walkthroughs

- Journal writing

- Demonstration lessons

- Pre/Post-observation conversations

- Online courses

- Web conferences

Professional Learning Structure	Who is participating?	What is the purpose?	When will it take place?	How will it take place?
Possibilities:	*Individual, group, pairs, teachers, administrators, district-level personnel, parents, community members, board of trustees, other*	*Gather information from external sources, look at student work, look into classrooms, focus on pedagogy, reflection, experience-based results in product, good for problem solving, promote dialogue, other*	*Frequency (daily, weekly, monthly, other), duration (more than three hours, one to two hours, less than one hour, other), in or out of school time, other*	*Internal facilitation, external facilitation, print resources required, budget required*
Peer coaching:	Pairs, teachers	Focus on pedagogy, reflection, look at student work, look into classrooms, good for problem solving, promote dialogue	Weekly, less than one hour during school time	No facilitator needed
Book study:	Groups, teachers, administrators	Gather information from external source, reflection, focus on pedagogy, promote dialogue	Weekly for four weeks, out of school time	Facilitated by internal consultant, each participant requires a copy of the book, small budget required for snacks

The Powerful Design Chart outline can be found as a reproducible on page 150 of appendix 2.

The list that they generated served as a kind of menu for selecting structures to support the outcomes of their professional development plan, their budget, internal expertise, and the needs of their learners. Structures were analyzed to best match the professional development experience to the participants' learning needs and context. (See sample Powerful Design Chart analysis above.)

A district's curriculum consultant team met to ensure that, as they were working with teachers, either in small or large groups or in more or less formal settings, they would consciously frame the work around phases of learning—*activate*, *acquire*, and *apply*.

- Teachers were asked to begin by reflecting on their current practice *(activate)*. By beginning with the learner rather than with content, later information could be linked to previous knowledge or experience.

- Teachers needed significant time for dialogue and discussion *(acquire)*. An article, a piece of student work, a lesson plan, or a strategy was used as the focus for conversation. Questions that opened and focused these conversations allowed teachers to examine and reflect on their day-to-day work.

- Teachers needed time to plan forward *(apply)*. Professional learning opportunities included time for planning and committing to next steps (see sample below).

Questions to ask in each of the phases of learning

Phase	Sample Questions
Activate	• What are your beliefs about student assessment? • What assessment practices do you believe are powerful? • What thinking about assessment have you engaged in recently?
Acquire	• In what way does the lesson incorporate assessment *for* learning? • How can the strategy be shifted to involve the student reflection? • In what ways does the piece of work provide evidence of a student's understanding? • What connections are you making between the article and your practice?
Apply	• Based on your learning today, what might you try in your classroom? • In what ways might you shift a current practice to be more closely aligned with assessment *for* learning? • What planning would you like to engage in? • What would you like to learn more about? • What resources could be helpful to you? • What do you want to take into your classroom tomorrow? • What might you do less of?

The Phases of Learning outline can be found as a reproducible on page 151 of appendix 2.

The curriculum consultant staff of one large urban school district worked with the constraints of shrinking professional development budgets by establishing school-based assessment leadership teams at each school. These teams included administrative, support services, and teacher representation. Over the course of three years, these leadership teams were brought together centrally in order to

deepen their understanding of assessment *for* learning principles. Capacity was built by focusing on content, providing suggestions regarding how to engage their local school staff in learning, and highlighting adult learning design, change theory, and coaching. These teams of teachers and administrators were provided with specific tools and strategies to support their leadership at the school level. Funding was allocated to allow for a member(s) of the school-based leadership team to meet with teachers, to work alongside teachers in their classrooms, and to structure alternative learning options for school staff.

Feedback for Learning Connections:

John Hattie researches and writes about how teachers can make a difference for student learning. Of particular interest is his work on feedback and retention. He has tracked research related to feedback and its impact on learning over a number of years. His findings help move us forward in terms of adult as well as student learning.

"*An investment in knowledge pays the best interest.***"**

Benjamin Franklin

Lessons Learned

- Differentiate approaches. Varied learning styles and multiple paths address the uniqueness of each adult learner and enable choice, while affirming the common destination.

- Begin with the end in mind. Identify broad learning goals at the beginning of your planning cycle and have them serve as a compass, as you build your professional development plan. Use them to guide the collection of evidence to document adult learning in support of evidence-based professional development.

- Create multilayered teams. Organize educators into both vertical and horizontal learning teams that meet on a regular basis and operate with a commitment to continuous learning and experimentation.

- Develop a plan for all members and groups of your community of learners—grade levels and/or departments, specialist teachers, school administrators, district office personnel, board of trustees, parents, individual school faculties, and paraprofessional staff—to grow together. Meeting with colleagues in similar and in different positions to learn, practice, and reflect prevents isolated pockets of learning and builds a common sense of purpose.

- Develop plans that are flexible and responsive. Build in opportunities for regular feedback and a willingness to adjust the course, based on the information collected, so the professional development plan doesn't become stale and irrelevant.

- Slow down to the speed of learning. Promote deep understanding.

- Model reflection, planning forward, and active construction of knowledge through interaction and practice that parallel the assessment *for* learning strategies that teachers are expected to use with their students.

- Frame learning with questions and experiences that push beyond single answers or a "right" strategy. Suggest multiple pathways that require consideration of the varied experiences, contexts, cultures, values, and unique challenges that all students bring into the classroom.

- Build networks and teams of teachers. Sharing within the community—no matter the size—informs and refines one another's practice. It is critical for teachers to have at least one other person to talk with in their own setting. Dedicated and energized professionals can lose momentum and commitment when faced with being the sole person in the building, level, department, or program who is expected to "infect" the rest of the staff. However, creating a formal team all the time isn't necessary. Sometimes simply talking with one person about misgivings and unexpected results can help an educator to confirm perceptions, to celebrate small successes, and to ask for assistance.

- Apply research. Educators need to become informed consumers of the research that supports the work in assessment *for* learning, while making connections to their own unique experiences and challenges.

- Allocate appropriate funds. Investing in release time for collaboration, team meetings, classroom observations, coaches, and external support results in long-term benefits.

- Gather information about what the adult learners know and what they still need to learn. Don't assume that you know this.

- Create a positive learning environment. Learning cannot take place in a milieu of misinformation, mistrust, and apprehension. Adults need to feel as if they can take risks with their learning and try out new ideas without fear of judgment or consequence.

- Plan with others. Talk with personnel in other districts or schools to learn what has worked for them as they planned for systemic professional development. Consulting with colleagues reveals both successes and missteps that can inform your actions.

As we plan for and implement professional learning, we are reminded to keep adult learners in mind—their strengths, experiences, and learning styles. We must provide them with choice, opportunities to learn and practice, as well as instructional methods that fit their way of constructing knowledge. At the same time, it is important to plan for the learning of the leaders; they need to learn and practice alongside their colleagues. Modeling is a powerful learning and teaching tool!

A cohesive, long-term, and textured plan that encourages sustainability of thought and practice reminds our communities and decision-makers that professional learning is worth the expense.

Professional Learning Resource Connections:

Learning Forward (formerly NSDC) is a nonprofit professional association that focuses on providing leadership, information, and research regarding effective professional development. Learning For-ward has created standards that guide informed decisions about meeting the learning needs of educators for results-driven, standards-based, and job-embedded professional development.

Task 1: As you consider your personal professional learning in relation to school and/or system learning needs in the area of assessment *for* learning, what structures may meet your needs? Using the reproducible on page 150 of appendix 2, consider each structure in the four areas of the Powerful Design Chart. Based on your analysis, what combination of structures will serve you best?

Name: S. Hall
Position: Grade 11 mathematics teacher
School: River High School

Outcomes: By the end of June, I will develop a professional portfolio that shows evidence of setting and using criteria with my students.

Connection to School, District, or State Plans: The school district has as one of its four priorities increasing student achievement by engaging students in assessment.

Strategies:
- Read a book and professional journal articles on setting and using criteria.
- Become a member of the school board assessment leadership committee.
- Attend district book study on assessment.
- Set criteria with students requiring two performance tasks per semester.
- Have students self-assess performance tasks using established criteria.
- Maintain a journal to reflect on setting and using criteria.
- Talk with colleagues in the school who have experience setting and using criteria with students.
- Include entries into portfolio (i.e., articles with reflection, lesson plans, session notes, student evidence).

Expected Student Outcomes:
- Increased student engagement in performance tasks.
- Increased student ability to provide specific, descriptive feedback to self and others.

Evidence of Success: (to be completed at the end of year)

An outline of this figure can be found as a reproducible on page 152 of appendix 2.

Task 2: Using the reproducible on page 151 of appendix 2, what activities and/or questions could your leadership team use as you move through the Phases of Learning?

Task 3: Using one of the two planning frames provided on pages 149 and 152 of appendix 2, develop your own professional growth plan related to increasing your understanding of assessment *for* learning.

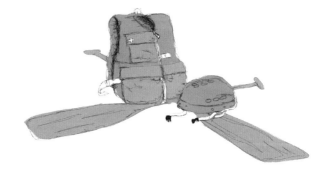

Expanding Proof
of Success

"Many of life's failures are people who did not realize how close they were to success when they gave up.""

Thomas A. Edison

We evaluate what we value. Systems define success in relation to their purpose and goals. If the measure of success is limited to only quantitative data, the destination may also become limited. What does your system value? What do you evaluate? Are the indicators of success appropriate, and do they include evidence of learning from multiple sources collected over time? How can you use assessment *for* learning to provide evidence of working towards or achieving your mission?

Leaders—whether teachers, principals, directors, or superintendents—need to work with learners to define the learning destination, to list all possible evidence, and to define success. This process does more than simply inform everyone. It provides time to build a common understanding of success. Done well, it enhances relationships and creates a common purpose.

Remember, *we evaluate what we value.* Therefore, if we collect simple, comparative numerical data, we communicate that we value that which can be measured simply and in numerical terms. We end up doing what Paul LeMahieu (1996) warns us against—we end up *accounting* for learning rather than *being accountable* for it. Alfred North Whitehead reminds us that what is needed is the kind of "simplicity that is found on the far side of complexity." When we begin with complexity and move towards something that is simple and easy to use in comparison, we can meet the need to be thorough while honoring the complexity of the task, as well as meeting the needs of the varied audiences.

How is this done? Let's begin with complexity: we begin with the end in mind—that is, what needs to be learned. We will use the classroom assessment process as an example and then illustrate how it works at the school and district levels.

A Classroom Accountability Process

Teachers have learners whom they need to coach towards success. This requires them to begin with the learning standards or outcomes they are required to teach and that students need to learn. They are accountable for teaching to the standards. The measure of a teacher's success is students' learning.

Assessment Plan
4th Grade
Mathematics—Problem Solving

Destination	Evidence of Learning / Proof
• Students will know what the learning targets are • Solve problems using more than one strategy • Justify answers and solution processes • Articulate their thinking in writing • Identify mathematical operations and strategies to solve problems	• Kids demonstrating a process of strategy (kids showing kids) • Problem-solving growth over time • Journals • Please notice . . . put on work • Self-assessment • Conversations • Observation of hands-on activities
Samples / Models	**Assessments / Evaluations**
• Exemplars (why this is a good problem) • Variety of problem-solving strategies • Shared work • Class brainstormed criteria	• Communicates effectively. Connects ideas to self, to others, and to tasks • Applies concepts, skills, and strategies to solve problems • Articulates clear understandings of concepts being studied • Understands and applies mathematical concepts being studied • Test and quiz scores—80 to 100% • Rubric scores—3s and 4s on 4-point scale

Thank you to colleagues in Maine.

Here are the steps in the classroom assessment process:

Step One:
Teachers review the learning standards or outcomes of the course or grade level. Then they group and summarize them, expressing them in simple language that students and parents can understand. This is the *learning destination.*

Step Two:
Teachers list all the possible evidence of the learning destination. They consider all the student work products, the conversations, and the observations that could be proof of learning. It is essential to consider all sources and list all evidence.

Step Three:
Teachers consider the available models or samples of what success looks like and collect those that are needed. They make plans to collect further samples over time.

Step Four:
Teachers describe what it would look and sound like to achieve high levels of success. This is the definition that will define the terms used to communicate levels of success and help guide growth over time.

A sample of the classroom assessment process is shown in the figure on the facing page. So what does it look like for leaders at other levels of the education system? Three examples follow.

Teacher Evaluation

As teachers coach students, school principals also need to coach staff members towards success. One principal met with teachers and had them respond to the question: "What is important when teaching the range of students in our school?" They brainstormed a list together. They considered past experience as well as criteria of excellence in teaching provided by professional bodies that certify teachers (i.e., National Board Certification in the United States or Provincial Certification Boards in Canada). They reviewed the research in terms of what makes for excellence in teaching. They built the most comprehensive list possible, with a great diversity of ideas represented. Similar ideas were grouped together. Then they summarized the groups of ideas by expressing them in easy-to-understand phrases. This became the content of their T-chart: the learning destination description.

At the next meeting, they listed all the possible evidence for each criterion of the learning destination. They examined products, conversations, and observations—anything that could be considered proof. The principal prompted by asking questions such as: "What would you see if you spent time observing in the classroom?" "What would you hear?" "What would students say?" "What would parents say?" They considered all sources and listed all possible evidence.

Before the principal embarked on a teacher's evaluation, the teacher and principal revisited the co-constructed criteria, talked about strengths, and reviewed the teacher's professional goals. The principal made a series of observations. Then they met and brought along a range of evidence, discussed what the evidence signified, and set plans for future professional growth. From these multiple sources of evidence—products, observations, and focused conversations—the principal wrote the teacher's evaluation.

What does effective teaching look like and sound like? (DRAFT)

Learning Destination	Examples of Possible Evidence
• Create a safe and positive learning environment for all. • Teach with intentionality and purpose. • Use ongoing assessment information to fine-tune instruction. • Engage learners in assessment *for* learning. • Demonstrate and use knowledge of learners and learning. • Respond to individual differences by adjusting teaching practices. • Evaluate students based on evidence of learning. • Model lifelong learning.	Includes observations, products, and conversations: • Classroom procedures and routines, such as class meetings, cooperative learning, peer-to-peer interaction • Written lesson plans—plans aligned with standards • Goals posted, understandings posted, essential questions posted • Students can articulate purpose and intention • Variety of assessment methods: pre-, ongoing, post-, self-assessments, peer assessments, performance tasks • Students are involved in co-constructing criteria • Using differentiated instructional strategies • Walkthroughs to collect evidence • Self-assessments / reflections • More . . .
Models, Exemplars, Samples	**Evaluation and Reporting**
• Lesson plans differentiated • Video of co-constructing criteria with class • Video of classroom routines • Lab/Classroom observations • Samples of visual rubrics • Example of professional development plan • Sample assessments • Learning inventories • Interest inventories • Student work samples	• Need to make an informed professional judgment based on policy

Thanks to colleagues in Honolulu, Hawaii, and Concord, New Hampshire, for this draft.

One superintendent met with all principals and vice principals and asked them to respond to the question: "What is important when providing outstanding professional leadership in our schools?" They brainstormed a list together, putting each item on a strip of chart paper. They referred to research summaries related to excellence in school-based leadership. They took time during two different meetings to build a comprehensive list. Participants grouped similar ideas together and summarized the content in each group of ideas, expressing them in simple phrases. Finally, they built a four-pocket portfolio and talked about all the possible evidence for each element of the learning destination. They considered different sources and kinds of evidence, asking: "What products, conversations, and observations could be proof of learning and from whom could they be collected?" (See figure below.)

What makes an effective leader? (DRAFT)

Learning Destination	Examples of Possible Evidence

1. Nurture the vision and demonstrate effective leadership qualities.
2. Foster strong learning communities and feed-forward so everyone and every part of the system learns.
3. Be supportive, engaged, and use highly developed interpersonal skills.
4. Be a high-quality teacher as you:
  • Create a safe and positive learning environment for all
  • Teach with intentionality and purpose
  • Use ongoing assessment information to fine-tune instruction
  • Engage learners in assessment *for* learning
  • Demonstrate and use knowledge of learners and learning
  • Respond to individual differences by adjusting teaching practices
  • Evaluate learners based on evidence of learning
  • Model lifelong learning
	• 360-degree feedback surveys from all staff, parents, trustees, students, and community members
	• Strong, effective leadership team as evidenced by interview
	• Self-assessments
	• Peer assessments
	• Progress towards vision
	• Retention of staff
	• Products such as reports, meeting minutes, student achievement results
	• Complaints and grievances
	• Professional learning opportunities (as leader and as participant)
	• Evidence of good health and balanced life (self-assessment / fitness test results)
	• Professional growth plans for school leaders modeled after professional growth plans for other staff
	• Evidence of effective job coaching of others
	• And more . . .

Thanks to colleagues in Honolulu, Hawaii, and Concord, New Hampshire, for this draft.

A group of people involved in a variety of roles in professional development met and took time to set criteria. They used a simple process: working from a brainstormed list to grouping similar ideas and then posting them on a criteria chart. Once it was complete, they shared the list and used it to guide their work in professional learning. Another group decided it was important that they have agreed-upon ways to work with one another. They brainstormed the list of key ideas, which were grouped, sorted, and posted (see figure below).

Criteria for Working Together	Details / Specifics	
Be encouraging	- stay positive / on task - encourage all learners - be a cheerleader! - positive, supportive feedback - be encouraging	- encourage each other - be positive!! - stay positive
Take turns and contribute	- establish roles - participate - one person talking at a time - take turns / no monopolizing - participate! - keep the end in mind - stay on topic - stay on topic - take turns	- take turns reporting - everyone contributes ideas - take turns doing all the roles - take turns - Ground Rules: take turns speaking, reporting, recording - communicate - stay focused - ask lots of questions - take turns - take turns
Listen for understanding	- listen to each other - ask for clarification - clarify and understand - listen and try to understand what others are saying - Rules: listen actively - listen with an open mind	- good listeners - Ground Rules: listen to each other - listen - active listening - pass on thinking - active listening - Ground Rules: listening to each other—listen to understand (questioning)
Be respectful of yourself and others	- be time conscious - have an open mind - value all opinions - respect the fact that to some people the glass is half empty - don't point fingers - okay to make mistakes - respect all group members - no put-downs - being non-judgmental, accepting and supportive - positive body language	- Ground Rules: respect each other and their opinions - listen respectfully - non-judgmental / respect differences - consider all ideas - keep an open mind - respect diverse teaching levels and different wants and needs - respect everyone's opinions - accept all spellings—without corrections - acceptance of disagreement (validate all opinions) - respect different ideas—agree to disagree
Have fun	- enjoy each other - fun is allowed - humor	- fun - humor is allowed and encouraged

Once learners know the learning destination, then everyone can begin to collect evidence of working towards it and achieving success. Learners can self-assess in relation to the agreed-upon learning destination and set goals. Leaders can support learners to reach their learning goals. Everyone can collect evidence over time, meeting periodically to review the evidence and decide on next steps. At this point, the "simplicity that can be found on the far side of complexity" is a reality. As learners set goals and collect evidence of growing towards excellence, they can be working harder than the teacher or coach and their learning can increase.

"Your true value depends entirely on what you are compared with."

Bob Wells

Evidence of Learning Connections:

Paul LeMahieu, currently senior partner for design, development, and research at the Carnegie Foundation, has researched and written extensively about portfolios and accounting for learning. His work has assisted us to see how portfolios can be productively used as part of a body of evidence for large-scale assessment, as well as to inform classroom assessment.

Diversity–Evidence Connection:

Beverly Farr and Elise Trumbull have researched and written extensively about the challenges of assessment equity in our diverse classrooms. They raise critical questions about assessments that limit students' ability to show proof of learning in their book, *Assessment Alternatives for Diverse Classrooms* (1997). Affirming that "cultural and linguistic diversity bring with them diversity in cognitive and communicative styles and strategies . . . The rush to [assessment] sameness can result in failure to draw upon students' particular strengths and ways of knowing" (1997, pp. 15–16).

- Share ownership and build understanding. When we articulate the destination together, we build the shared understandings of the evidence we need in order to move forward.

- Model good teaching and learning practices. When leaders deliberately use assessment *for* learning strategies to help people learn more prior to assessment *of* learning, two benefits emerge: people learn more and leaders model good practice. It is important that leaders and learners work together to describe what success looks like. When we begin with the end in mind, we find out what learners already know and what they need to know. We give learners time to learn. As they learn, they produce evidence that shows growth towards excellence.

- Gather evidence from multiple sources over time. When we triangulate our evidence and collect it over time, valuing both qualitative and quantitative evidence of learning, we can be confident that our findings are reliable and valid. We are then able to share our findings, using evidence that people value.

- Plan to collect both qualitative and quantitative measures of success. Proof of successful implementation includes data from conversations, work products, discussions, reflections, and anecdotes. If quantitative data are required for purposes of executive summary and reporting, then qualitative data can be encoded—summarized into numbers or symbols.

As you can see, this process supports us as we seek to evaluate what we value. Success is defined in relation to purpose and goals, and in language everyone understands. The evidence is varied and recognized in the complexity of the work being done to support learners. Everyone can use assessment *for* learning to learn more.

Assessment Plan (DRAFT) for: Grade Level:	
Destination	**Evidence of Learning**
What does it look like and sound like to be successful at the end of the year?	What evidence will the learner have? How can the learner show his/her learning to others?
Samples / Models	**Evaluation**
What samples, exemplars, or anchors do you have that show quality? (They need to reflect a range.) For what evidence do you need to involve the learner in setting the criteria?	How will you know you are successful? What evidence will your professional judgment be based on?

An outline of this figure can be found as a reproducible on page 153 of appendix 2.

Using the frame provided as a reproducible on page 153 of appendix 2, create a plan to assess your work in the classroom, school, or district based on the steps in the classroom assessment process:

- *Destination:* What does it look like and sound like to be successful at the end of the year?

- *Evidence of Learning:* What evidence will the learner have? How can the learner show his/her learning to others?

- *Samples/Models:* What samples, exemplars, or anchors do you have that show quality? (These need to reflect a range.) For which evidence do you need to involve the learner in setting the criteria?

- *Evaluation/Assessment of Learning:* How will you know you are successful? What evidence will your professional judgment be based on?

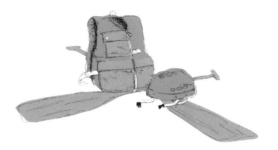

Moving From Resistance to Support

"Everyone wants improvement; it's change that they don't like."

Anonymous

Leading change requires us to be prepared to embrace resistance. Resistance can be fueled in many ways. For example, those who resist may:

- Not understand the research behind assessment *for* learning

- Think the time is not right

- Need to understand what the change looks like

- Feel less than competent in the face of this change

- Be afraid to take risks or lose control

- Not understand how the change will be managed

- Wonder how assessment *for* learning will impact students and parents

This sampling of different concerns demonstrates the need for leaders to respond and act in different ways.

If it is so difficult to change habits and behaviors, how can we overcome resistance as we move forward with assessment *for* learning at every part of the system, from individuals to communities to organizations? Sometimes people are simply waiting for a compelling reason to change.

Resistance is a natural part of change; today's leaders work *with* resistance, not against it. Today's resistance is potentially tomorrow's support. In fact, leaders reframe resistance by viewing it rather as a continuum of readiness (Tschannen-Moran and Tschannen-Moran 2010). Here are some ways leaders do this important work:

> The departments of a small high school were applying the principles of assessment *for* learning to the classroom through a cycle of planning, practice, reflection, and adjustment. A staff member was refusing to engage in this work, and her conversations were making others feel that the work was not important. The principal spoke with the staff member and indicated to her that while she could choose not to participate at this time, she could not continue to hamper the work of the teams. The principal also assured her that he would support her transition into the work when she felt that she was ready to join the team.

> A superintendent of a small urban school district reflected on the times when he felt resistant to an initiative of change. He made his thinking public as he spoke with school administrators about the assessment *for* learning focus. He legitimized personal concerns and feelings through the anecdotes he shared. At the same time, he provided the administrators with strategies for dealing with resistant feelings among the school staff.

> A superintendent's department of a school district that had identified assessment *for* learning as a priority expected all schools to include a school-based goal regarding assessment in their school plan. Realizing that resistance can grow when parameters are tightly defined, the superintendent celebrated the diversity of each plan. Some schools looked at assessment *for* learning through the lens of literacy, while others focused on ways in which to involve students in sharing their learning. Other schools committed to setting criteria with students in content areas, while still others examined the connection between self-assessment and goal setting. The element of choice allowed schools to satisfy the expectations. By not expecting all work to look, sound, and feel the same, resistance was minimized.

> An elementary school principal prepared a "menu" of learning opportunities. Her experience had shown that a powerful way to reduce resistance is through choice and differentiation of professional

development. Staff can choose to learn in small groups, attend seminars and workshops, participate in a book study, or go to another school to observe lessons. In this way, the teachers know that the administrator respects their differences and honors their unique learning styles. (See pages 51 and 52 for more options.)

A high school principal heard about the experience of a second-year high school teacher in a neighboring community who was a member of a professional learning community that did not meet. When she tried asking her team members to get together, they were always too busy. Her next step was to ask the school principal for assistance. His advice was to tell them to meet. The result? The second-year teacher did not get the kind of professional learning support that was required and longed for. As a result of hearing this story, the high school principal set norms of collaboration (Costa and Garmston 1994) with the entire staff prior to beginning PLCs. Then, at every staff meeting everyone was part of checking in with these norms. Every PLC also began and ended with a check-in with the school's norms of collaboration. In this way, the principal had implemented a structure that would minimize the possibility of what had happened to the second-year teacher being repeated at his school.

The principal of a large middle school incorporated 30 minutes of professional learning about assessment *for* learning on each staff meeting agenda. This sometimes included watching a video segment, reading a brief article, or examining a sample of student work. Regardless of the format, the majority of the time was spent in professional dialogue. Through observation, she realized that those individuals who struggled to include students in their assessment often did not participate in the structured large-group conversation. As a result, the staff was divided into smaller groups of three staff members each. These staff members were not on the same teaching team and did not typically work on a daily basis with one another. This close format naturally encouraged all people to become involved in the interaction and offered perspectives that challenged the thinking of each team member.

An assistant superintendent brought together school-based assessment leadership teams to share the district's vision and action plan around assessment *for* learning, the process that was used to identify both, and the reasons why assessment *for* learning was selected as a focus. The session included significant time for the participants to deal with the information, provide feedback, and ask questions. The process that would be used to consider the feedback at the district level was provided. If a question could not be answered, the assistant superintendent indicated that he would find the answers. A week after the session, a bulletin was distributed to all participants with the collated feedback, the revisions to the shared vision and action plan, and responses to the questions posed. The transparency of the process and the promised follow-up and responses signaled to the staff and to those who were struggling to make connections to the district's focus that honesty and responsiveness would be a cornerstone of the work ahead.

A school principal recognized that a couple of staff members were struggling to participate in learning experiences about assessment *for* learning principles and strategies. As a result, she examined her own role in leading the work over the past few months. At subsequent staff meetings, she asked teachers who were well respected on campus to share their attempts, successes, and failures in trying to engage students in assessment *for* learning. The voice of a valued colleague replaced that of the positional leader and allowed people who were resisting the opportunity to hear from respected teaching colleagues.

A middle school principal observed that a team of teachers was disillusioned with the direction of the school in having students create portfolios to communicate their learning. They spoke of waiting until this "bandwagon" finally passed by. It was important to the principal to learn why these teachers were resisting this work. He invited them to meet with him and, in an open and honest way, asked them to talk about their beliefs and feelings. The conversation, though difficult at first, began to flow once the teachers saw that he was not countering their statements with rebuttals. Instead, the principal took time to paraphrase both the emotion and content of their words. "Seeking to understand rather than be understood" allowed him to consider new points of view. In some cases, the problems proved easy to solve. For example, some of the necessary resources (professional books, videos, and articles) were difficult to locate. The principal added them to the staff library. For others, the issues were more complicated, like the response of parents to the use of portfolios. For these issues, the principal built consensus around effective action by involving all teachers in the conversation.

An assistant superintendent of a large school district recognized that a strong communication strategy was essential to minimize resistance during the implementation of a plan to increase student achievement through assessment *for* learning. All school administrators met together only a few times each year; however, the administrators of each level (early, middle, and senior) gathered once a month. As part of that meeting, an update was provided that highlighted the work of the district assessment steering committee and of each level. This information kept everyone feeling connected and in the loop.

A district assessment leadership team created a multiyear implementation plan focusing on increasing educators' understanding of assessment *for* learning principles. To include input from a broad cross section of the district, each school identified a representative to meet with the committee and provide feedback on behalf of the whole school. This process took some time; however, the team knew that it was important to allow many voices to be heard. As people were engaged in the decision-making process, resistance was reduced.

An elementary school principal led his staff through a process of reflection on a district assessment policy that codified the principles of assessment *for* learning and assessment *of* learning. As part of the conversation, he asked the staff to brainstorm a list of reasons that they could imagine hearing from others about why it would be difficult to implement the policy. Following a strategy to prioritize these statements of resistance, he modeled the creation of talking points to respond to the possible difficulties that might emerge. These points were used in conversations between themselves and others.

"You will never stub your toe by standing still. The faster you go, the more chance there is of stubbing your toe, but the more chance you have of getting somewhere."

Charles F. Kettering

Lessons Learned

- Embrace resistance. Though this seems almost contradictory, it is important to learn about what causes educators to resist. In identifying the themes and patterns of resistance, we can create new possibilities that meet the needs of people who are resisting a change. Further, sometimes we discover that the people who are resisting inform the work in important ways.

- Reframe resistance from the notion of "I won't" to one of "I can't." In this way, resistance is shifted to reluctance.

- Assume a stance of positive intent. We need to recognize that teachers and others are doing the best they can do with what they currently know. We lose nothing of ourselves as leaders when we respect those who resist, and are sensitive to and plan for their points of view.

- Build relationships. Know the people with whom you work. Your staff has learning needs no different than the students you used to teach. It is important that they know you care and are open to their viewpoints. In this way, they will share their concerns directly with you, without the need to go underground.

- Be clear about what's in it for them. Identify how assessment *for* learning can save time, reduce discipline problems, and increase the achievement of all students, particularly for those who struggle. These are compelling reasons for staff to become genuinely engaged.

- Maintain your cool and keep your emotions in check. Though sometimes your level of frustration may be high, remember that your colleagues are closely monitoring your reactions to those who put up roadblocks. Refrain from speaking negatively to others about people who are resisting. Though it may be tempting to share thoughts and opinions about those who resist the work at hand and make it difficult to move forward, it is essential to maintain a professional attitude, monitoring our own reactions and emotions.

- Persevere. It is important to maintain the compelling vision of what is possible. While we consider the thinking of those who resist and plan ways to support their learning, we cannot stop the work in which the majority of staff is engaged.

Working Through Resistance

• **What is happening? What is the situation? What is going on here?**
A group of teachers with whom I am working continue to say that there is no time in their day to involve students in their own assessment. There is too much to do and so this is an extra that they cannot support.

• **What is my/our personal reaction to this?**
Each time I hear someone say this, I really get frustrated. I know that it can work, and, in fact, I have done this in my classroom. The research in this area is so powerful. It also saddens me that the attitude of either/or cannot be shifted.

• **Why do I/we think that this is happening?**
I think that these teachers are feeling this way because they do not have a mental picture of what it can look like. The practical strategies are still in the abstract form for them. Also, I wonder how the group's thoughts impact the whole. Is there an individual who may think otherwise, but is afraid to voice his opinion because of what others might say?

• **What may be some consequences if this continues?**
If we cannot move beyond the thinking that this can't happen, we have really stalled in our work together. If the abstract cannot become practical, how will future learning and direction be impacted?

• **What am I/are we willing to do about it? What will my/our initial response be?**
Perhaps I should involve a couple of these teachers in observing someone from another school that is similar in its demographics. This may put a strong image in their minds. Also, we could show them a couple of short video clips of classroom teachers involving students in their assessment. I think that I also need to ask them again what would be helpful to them and reframe my commitment of support. There must be one teacher who is willing to attempt something.

• **How can I/we manage my/our personal reaction?**
I need to remember to not take their comments personally and I need to remind myself of the occasions when it took me more time to deeply understand a practice. Speaking to one of my colleagues and asking her how she deals with resistance could be additional learning for me.

An outline of this figure can be found as a reproducible on page 154 of appendix 2.

We need the tools to plan for resistance and the strategies to deal with resistance. In both cases, leaders work to remove the reasons why educators are not engaged in the important work around assessment *for* learning. When the reasons to be resistant are minimized, critical mass builds, resulting in deep learning for both teachers and students. The figure on page 75 called Working Through Resistance illustrates the reflective thinking of a leader who takes stock of resistance and determines how to respond productively.

Task for the Leadership Team

Making a plan to work with resistance is critical to implementing change. Look at the example titled Working Through Resistance on page 75. Using the reproducible on page 154 of appendix 2 as a template, consider a situation in which you are encountering or have encountered resistance. Reflect on that situation using the following questions:

- What is happening? What is the situation? What is going on here?

- What is my/our personal reaction to this?

- Why do I/we think that this is happening?

- What may be some consequences if this continues?

- What am I/are we willing to do about it? What will my/our initial response be?

- How can I/we manage my/our personal reaction?

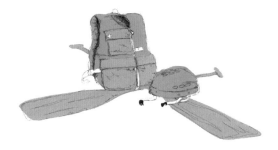

Bridging the
Implementation Dip

"Pressure means ambitious targets. Support involves developing new competencies. The more that pressure and support become seamless, the more effective the change process will be at getting things to happen."

Michael Fullan

Contents

We know that when we implement a new initiative, there are those who embrace it with high levels of enthusiasm. We also know that some will be reluctant. And yet, as we move forward, there is enough momentum, support, curiosity, and goodwill to leave the shore. But what we also know is that we should not expect instant success. In fact, just downriver, what we should actually expect is what experts have called the "implementation dip"—that is, ". . . literally a dip in performance and confidence as one encounters an innovation that requires new skills and new understandings" (Fullan 2001, p. 40).

The implementation dip is exactly that—a dip or a drop in performance, results, or commitment. It might be that some have not yet given up former ways of being or doing things. Or it might be that some have not yet mastered new strategies; the skills and understanding have not yet been solidified. Or it might be that some are scared of what is new. In any case, as leaders we must recognize and anticipate the implementation dip, and we should appreciate that it could take us off course if we are not mindful of ways to deal with it.

When we use assessment *for* learning as the bridge to success, the implementation dip does not prove to be disastrous, because it increases sustainability of the initiative. Here are two powerful ways to use assessment *for* system learning as a bridge to sustainability.

Specific Feedback to Provide Pressure and Support

Whenever school systems shift priorities or focus, they tend to look to their staff development personnel to engage the teaching community in learning more about it. This takes place in a variety of ways and formats. However, after initial opportunities to explore these ideas, strategies, or conceptual frameworks, difficult questions, resistance, reluctance, and policy issues begin to surface. It seems as though success is about to once more prove elusive. Yet, research shows there is an error in our actions and it is this: professional development personnel cannot take the sole lead on this important work. When the responsibility of teaching the adults in the system resides with the professional development experts alone, the authority and ability to respond to the pushback, which inevitably emerges, does not typically lie with them. It lies with those who have positional leadership; those who are responsible for the quality of the instruction and for student learning and are entrusted with providing instructional leadership.

When the implementation appears to be at risk or failing, then both pressure and support are needed (Fullan 2001). The role of "support" is to invite learning. It comes from many sources, including from those who are providing the professional development. Pressure is different. It is needed when a shift in practice is required. Pressure typically comes from someone who is in a supervisory role—such as a principal or a superintendent.

Let us reframe this idea from the perspective of Peter Senge (2006), who noted that ongoing reflective feedback was needed if ongoing learning and progress were going to occur—in other words, feedback that invites learning while *requiring* change. It is feedback that comes from those in supervisory roles (line authority). Experience has shown that the role of feedback in adult learning depends on the relationship between the giver and the receiver. If feedback is going to support the learning of people who are choosing to change as well as those who may, for many different reasons, be reluctant to change, then it must come from multiple sources (supervisory staff as well as professional development staff) over time. Because of this, if the responsibility for the learning initiative is placed solely in the hands of the professional development staff, then the initiative will experience failure and not recover from the dip. The implementation dip is only bridged if practice (on the part of everyone involved) actually changes. That can only happen when ongoing feedback is continually received from those in supervisory roles. Therefore, those in supervisory positions need to be, and be seen to be, working and learning alongside those who are providing the professional learning (see figure below). This is a significant part of instructional leadership. That is, this specific, ongoing feedback, in the form of both pressure and support, must come simultaneously if the implementation dip is to be bridged.

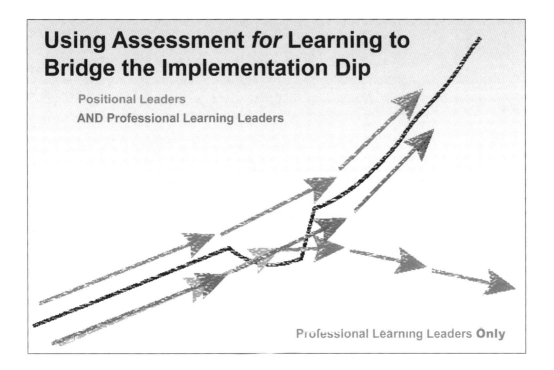

Using Assessment *for* Learning to Bridge the Implementation Dip

Positional Leaders
AND Professional Learning Leaders

Professional Learning Leaders **Only**

It is often said that change happens when you see the next step. In this work, it is important that people are both supported and pressured to take concrete and informed next steps. Just as student learners share evidence of their learning with others, adult learners need to do the same. However, the pace at which this public and participatory learning takes place is an important decision, and a wise leader will move forward only after a careful assessment of the group and its strength as a supportive learning community. The expectations of the types of evidence that will be shared, along with the choice of audience, move, over time, from safe, close, and familiar to more risky and further away. If the adult learning community is not yet strong (i.e., having respectful, shared norms of collaboration, shared language, shared vision, and so on), the speed of making learning public will need to be adjusted while the relationships among group members are strengthened.

For example, a group of principals is learning to co-construct criteria.

- The first time they do so it is as participants at a gathering of principals led by district leadership. As they leave, they are asked to provide feedback in the form of an exit slip—what does this process remind them of, what is one thing that they remember, and what is one question that they might have.

- The next time they come back together, the process is modeled once more and they talk with those they feel most comfortable with about their understandings of co-constructing criteria and share connections that they might have. They also understand that before they come back together for a third time, they will need to co-construct criteria with a group of their choice.

- When they arrive back together, they are asked to share their experience with someone else in the room (self-selected audience). At the end of this session, they are asked to once again identify how and when they are going to practice co-constructing criteria, and this time the groups are created so they know to whom they are going to show evidence when they return (selected audience).

Over time, the opportunity to practice co-constructing criteria increases (gradual release of responsibility) and the audience with whom the evidence is shared is larger and more unknown (increases personal risk). Notice that this way of structuring the learning provides an opportunity to share the evidence of learning (see figure below). All levels of leadership are informed through the examination of evidence of learning collected from multiple sources over time (triangulation). The visible presence of positional leaders (able to provide both pressure and support) is essential to the success of this work.

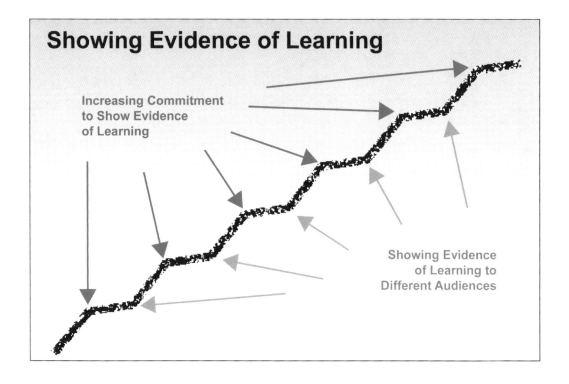

Showing Evidence of Learning

Increasing Commitment
to Show Evidence
of Learning

Showing Evidence
of Learning to
Different Audiences

"Leadership is as much about doing in order to think as thinking in order to do."

Henry Mintzberg

- When individuals in positions of leadership use assessment *for* learning strategies in their work in schools, implementation success is enhanced and sustainability becomes more likely.

- Successful implementation of assessment *for* learning initiatives is made possible when deliberate instructional leadership is planned, implemented, and continually supported over time by all levels of positional leadership in the school or system.

- Sustainable implementation occurs when the rituals and routines of an organization incorporate assessment *for* learning, including evidence-based feedback to feed-forward the learning on a continuous basis.

Assessment *for* Learning Implementation Connections:

John Gardner, a professor of education at Queen's University, Belfast, his colleague Ruth Leitch, and others have carried out a study of students' perceptions of the use of AFL approaches. Another study (with Assessment Reform Group colleagues) has been looking at recent large-scale projects across the UK and how changing assessment practices have been achieved or not achieved through those projects.

Task for the Leadership Team

Using the "staircase visual" on page 81, think about:

- In what ways do you invite educators across your system to provide evidence of their learning? Teachers? Administrators? District personnel?

- Over time, what do you ask them to share? With whom do you ask them to share their evidence?

- How do you support positional leaders to be effective instructional leaders using assessment *for* learning?

Involving Parents and Community

"School leadership needs to be a broad concept that is separated from person, role, and a discrete set of individual behaviors. It needs to be embedded in the school community as a whole. Such broadening of the concept of leadership suggests shared responsibility for a shared purpose of community."

Linda Lambert

Contents

It is not enough that parents and community be informed; they must be invited into the thinking and visioning that will provide the foundation for all that comes. They can become some of the most powerful advocates for thoughtful change when their resistance, concerns, and questions are dealt with honestly and respectfully. How can we help trustees, parents, and our communities to be part of the change? How can we use assessment *for* learning to guide this work?

Bridging home to school and school to home, inviting the broader community into the school, and learning from and with the folks in your area are important pursuits. Yet, none of these are easy. While many educators embrace this challenge, others do not yet appreciate the importance of building relationships with those outside the school building. They wonder why we need to engage those who have not had formal educational training in conversations about student learning. Some educators see themselves as the experts and believe the involvement of outsiders just slows things down. Yet other educators feel that inviting community members into the school requires them to justify everything that they do, and they become defensive and protective. To believe that parents and community cannot be part of the decision making or the direction setting is to minimize both their contributions and the school's success. Together is indeed better.

Moreover, some parents and community members have not had good school experiences themselves; they are anxious and nervous about becoming more involved in the life of the school. Many believe that it is not their place to enter into the educational dialogue even though they may have much to offer. Some are intimidated because they view themselves as uninformed in comparison to those with degrees in education. And for yet others, their lives are so tightly focused on making ends meet, working two jobs, or managing a tight schedule of activities, there may not be time left for engaging more fully in their child's education.

It is important to note that parents' silence does not simply equate to tacit approval. From our perspective, we may have put multiple structures and processes into place to invite and engage them. It may seem as if they are not interested in working with the school. However, what may hold them back can be far deeper. For some, their reality speaks to a true diversity of need. For example, the culture of poverty is a powerful force that can define each interaction and response. For others, a lack of involvement may be symptomatic of the exhaustion of feeling misunderstood, or the sense of separation that diversity of language, culture, and experience brings. Bringing an entire community together in a respectful and responsible way is a key strategy.

As educators, we must persist. Parents and community members are entitled to participate in the work of educating their children. This is a community's collective goal. Therefore, it is important that they, too, understand the role of assessment *for* learning in increasing student achievement, so that they can help to inform and advocate for policy and practice. In addition, parents and community members constitute a large part of the audience for assessment *of* learning results. They should have the tools to know what those results represent and how they are valued.

Research tells us that successful schools and successful leaders find ways to share information with and get information from those outside of the school as they work to create understanding together. Partnerships that will foster and promote this stance are not easy to forge; however, they are vitally important. We must consciously build structures of reciprocal learning and nurture relationships founded on trust and rapport. As we go about our work, we may be excluding others without intending to do so. Making the effort to welcome and include all people can bring an entire community together. This is hard work and often requires deep structural and procedural change on our part to uncover what we have unintentionally created over time.

Consider the following ways that schools have reached out to community members:

One middle school has students participate in end-of-the-year exit interviews. Students prepare a reflection of their learning over the year and present evidence of that learning to a small group of adults, consisting of a teacher, district personnel, parent representative, and a community member.

An elementary school holds student-parent-teacher conferences before the report card is prepared. The purpose of the conference is to jointly discuss the student's performance against the curricular standards/outcomes of the term. Evidence of the student's learning is used as a focal point for the conversations, and time is spent identifying next steps and setting goals. After this, the teachers write the report cards, incorporating the content of the conference as a guide for their thinking and evaluation.

An assistant superintendent of a large urban school district recognizes the shifting demographics of the community to include increasing numbers of First Nations' students and families. Acknowledging that she does not have the background or depth of knowledge to understand ways to genuinely and respectfully welcome and involve the Aboriginal community in the organizations of the schools and the district, she finds a well-respected Elder to guide and advise her. Through regular meetings and conversations, the assistant superintendent explores possibilities and strategies and ways of being that reflect the Aboriginal perspective. For example, meetings with Aboriginal families and students always take place in a circle and include an opportunity to smudge. These traditional structures are also incorporated across the schools so that Aboriginal students and their families can see themselves and their experiences in the everyday occurrences in the district.

A family of schools—four elementary, two middle, and one senior high—created a community action team. This team was comprised of not only educators and parents from each school, but also representatives from family services, the police, area businesses, health providers and clinics, recreation facilities, justice departments, housing departments, and senior citizen groups. The goal of this group was to coordinate services for the students of the area and to build connections between public and private sectors. Through the sharing of priorities by representatives, the entire group grew in their understanding of the work of the others. Issues were raised, and solutions were created. The schools consistently shared information regarding the work that they were all doing around assessment *for* learning and its link to student engagement and achievement.

An elementary school (students aged 5–13) planned a family math night. Parents and children worked through grade-level math activities and games that were set up in classrooms around the school. The activities reflected different curricular standards and used easily accessible materials and manipulatives. Each one also included prompts for reflection and self-assessment. At the end of the evening, every family received a package of additional activities and games that could be played at home. Later in the year, the school held family nights on other topics such as reading, environment, and culture.

A middle school teacher and his students prepared a packet of student work samples from the preceding month. These packets were sent home, along with activity suggestions. Parents and students worked together over the next week, going through the samples and highlighting certain aspects of the work. There were also materials that encouraged the family to engage in activities or games to illustrate skills and concepts.

Family–Community Partnership Connections:

Joyce Epstein, director of the Center on School, Family, and Community Partnerships and the National Network of Partnership Schools, researches and writes about involving the community, school, and family partnerships. Her framework for "action teams" centers around helping all students succeed in school and in later life.

A school district hired home–school coordinators whose job was to liaise with parents in each school community. These positions were filled by community members and did not require any formal training in education. They worked to welcome new families into their communities and to run literacy programming that brought families into the school after hours. They were available to answer general programming and instructional questions for parents who preferred not to approach a member of the faculty. The coordinators served as advocates when parents wanted the support. They participated in the school planning cycle and all professional learning so that the voices of the parents and the community were always at the table and considered when decisions needed to be made.

A school district's new policy on assessment shifted to strongly include the principles of assessment *for* learning. In the development of that policy, two parent focus groups were established along with those of teachers and administrators. These focus groups provided feedback to the district policy development committee in order that changes could be considered. After the policy had been finalized, a plan for implementation included parent information evenings. These were held throughout the school district, at different times of the day and in different venues, including community offices and buildings. Because of the diverse community population, sessions were offered in three languages. Follow-up meetings took place at the school level, through the parent advisory council structure.

A school district expected that each school's planning committee include parent representation. It was not enough to simply share the yearly school plan with the parent advisory council. The parent representative participated in the planning process by identifying SMART goals, indicators of success, strategies, and data sources. In this way, the voice of the parent was included as the work of the school was planned for, acted upon, and reviewed.

A school board includes community and parent representation on each of its four standing committees—program, policy, finance, and technology. Representatives are chosen, based on a formal process of application and selection that includes attention to regional, cultural, and demographic diversity. The members have full voting privileges and in this way, work to shape the direction of the school district.

"Communication is a process of sharing experience until it becomes a common possession. It modifies the disposition of both parties who partake in it."

John Dewey

Culture–Involvement Connections:

Martha Allexsaht-Snider's research on working with parents across cultures, cited in *Bridging Cultures Between Home and School* (Trumbull et al. 2001) focuses on engaging parents through recognition of their useful knowledge. She urges schools to recognize that parent involvement activities are not just opportunities for schools to transmit knowledge to parents, but for parents to educate teachers and administrators as well.

Lessons Learned

- Include students in their assessment and learning. When students understand what they are learning, why they are learning it, what they can do, and what they need to do next, they become the greatest ambassadors of educational practice. As parents and community see learning through the eyes of their children, they better understand and support children and schools.

- Bring parents into the school along with their children. Hold an information evening for just parents, and some will attend. Build in time for interaction and learning together as a family, and participation will explode.

- Meet parents and community members in settings outside of school where they are comfortable, and you communicate tangibly that they are worth the effort of your coming to them.

- Create norms of collaboration. As we include parents and community members on committees and teams and in the process of decision making, it is important to set the stage for our cooperation and collaboration. Time spent doing this will provide all members with criteria for the ways in which the group will act and behave. This evens the playing field. (See figure below for norms of collaboration.)

- Use analogies and non-educational examples to explain concepts about teaching and learning. These are powerful tools to promote understanding for those not involved in the daily work of school.

The Seven Norms of Collaborative Work

Pausing: Pausing before responding or asking a question allows time for thinking and enhances dialogue, discussion, and decision making.

Paraphrasing: Using paraphrase helps members of the group to hear and understand each other as they formulate decisions.

Probing: Using gentle open-ended probes or inquiries such as, "Please say more about . . ." or "I'm curious about . . ." increases the clarity and precision of the group's thinking.

Putting ideas on the table: Ideas are the heart of a meaningful dialogue.

Paying attention to self and others: Meaningful dialogue is facilitated when each group member is conscious of self and of others, and is aware of not only what she/he is saying, but also how it is said and how others are responding.

Presuming positive intentions: Assuming that others' intentions are positive promotes and facilitates meaningful dialogue and eliminates unintentional put-downs.

Pursuing a balance between advocacy and inquiry: Pursuing and maintaining a balance between advocating a position and inquiring about one's own and others' positions help the group to become a learning organization.

Adapted from *The Adaptive School: A Sourcebook for Developing Collaborative Groups* by Garmston and Wellman, 2009. Used with permission.

This figure can be found as a reproducible on page 155 of appendix 2.

When we plan to build partnerships with parents and community members, we have much to gain. As we sustain these partnerships, we show that we care. It is in these relationships that we not only inform, but can *be* informed. Thinking is strengthened, as the voices of the community beyond the school are included in decision making; they may remind us of things that we had not considered. This helps us move from a place of relative *sameness* to a place of possibilities and innovation. And, more importantly, we can construct understanding together. The school then becomes a community cornerstone where the work of the school, including assessment *for* learning, is understood and supported.

Task for the Leadership Team

Working With Parents and Community

Example	Providing information	Receiving information	Making decisions / setting direction together
Community member participates as part of a group of adults who assess student end-of-year exit interviews		✓	✓
Student-parent-teacher conferences take place before report card is written	✓	✓	✓
Community action team	✓	✓	✓
Parents and students work together through a package of student work samples		✓	
Parent focus groups provide feedback to policy development	✓		
Parent representation on school planning committee			✓
Parent representation on school district committees			✓

An outline of this figure can be found as a reproducible on page 156 of appendix 2.

Using the reproducible on page 156 of appendix 2, list the ways in which your system/organization involves parents. Consider whether each instance is an example of providing information to, receiving information from, or jointly making decisions. Examine patterns that emerge, and consider questions that arise about the balance of communication to, from, and with parents.

Increasing Quality Feedback

" To get feedback is not to gather opinions about an act we have undertaken . . . [Rather] in systems thinking, feedback is a broader concept. It means any reciprocal flow of influence. **"**

Peter Senge

Contents

Educators are always in the midst of changing and improving—our work has been compared to repairing an airplane engine while in flight. We know we have to move slowly and persistently forward, but how do we know what's working and what's not? What can we do to keep on track and informed of our successes as well as the lurking dangers?

As leaders we need evidence—the right kind and balance of data and proof—to keep our assessment *for* learning initiatives on track. Data collection requires advanced planning. It is not enough to begin the process without a plan to adjust our actions in order to make them more effective. When we come to the end of each phase of the initiative, it isn't enough to find out then that we don't have the evidence needed to show the overall impact on learning. We must carefully consider what combination of diverse evidence we need to reveal the depth of implementation and point towards next steps. We must thoughtfully consider what kind of feedback, based on the information, will best build momentum and inspire others to take the risks required. It is easy to forget that without ongoing, quality feedback, system learning suffers.

Learners and systems engaged in learning need multiple sources of continuous feedback. One of the greatest challenges leaders face is expanding the sources, frequency, and specificity of feedback so that everyone in the system can be learning and adjusting constantly in response to a continuous flow of feedback/feed-forward information.

Balanced and timely system feedback permits leaders to know whether or not the desired change is on track. Leaders can sustain change when they consciously build in checkpoints that keep themselves and others informed of progress and problems during the process of system learning. This ongoing flow of specific, timely feedback is informing the next action when results are widely communicated. This kind of feedback not only sustains the change but helps to build momentum. Effective leaders make it their business to know the status of the desired change. When leaders are constantly informed by both qualitative data as well as quantitative data, they have the quality feedback they need to make good decisions quickly.

Assessment that supports ongoing learning requires that rich and diverse data be constantly collected, monitored, and shared. Leaders look for information that gives a balanced picture of what is effective and what is not, while sustaining and building momentum. Decisions are informed by data. Everyone needs to know what quality looks like. Everyone needs to collect evidence that is reliable and valid—that is, evidence collected over time from multiple sources. That means building in specific, timely, frequent feedback that informs next steps for each person and each part of the system. This will allow everyone to see what is working and what needs to be done differently.

Feedback for Learning Connections:

Ruth Butler's research (1987, 1988) examines the role of feedback in learning. The research compared marks only, comments only, and marks and comments combined. The group given comments only showed significantly greater learning gains.

Improving performance often means taking calculated risks and doing things differently. Leaders seek to balance the tensions that naturally occur between stability and desired change. Leaders focused on system learning steer change in the right direction, by considering a full range of evidence that could show the degree of implementation needed to make the change. Effective leaders coach people through the discomfort that occurs when they make mistakes and learn something new, as a result of building in feedback and feed-forward loops. When leaders publicly learn from the feedback and adjust their ongoing work, they communicate by their actions that change is a process, not an event, and that feedback from our mistakes is the only route to greater success.

Leaders must establish systems that are aligned, structured, and comprehensive for collecting, monitoring, and communicating results in a way that is specific and that informs everyone's next steps. Leaders balance pressure and support. They successfully attend to these challenges in different ways as evidenced by the examples below:

> One urban district makes use of a balanced scorecard (or annual report) to communicate internally and externally about their progress toward meeting agreed-upon success targets, based on both quantitative and qualitative data. The scorecard reports progress on a set of four goal areas: 1) Student Learning; 2) Organizational Support and Improvement (finance, student and school support, information); 3) Human Resources—Learning and Growth (employment, training, support, compensation); and 4) Customers and Stakeholders (engagement, loyalty, satisfaction). Each goal area contains a carefully selected set of measures that communicate the district's performance in this area. The superintendent holds all members of the team accountable for setting these measures, collecting evidence linked to them, and periodically reviewing evidence on established intervals with the larger group for informed system decision making (see figure on page 94).

> Some school districts establish indicators of success across broad areas, such as student achievement, school safety, behavior management, graduation rates, and budgeting. Biannually, a committee meets to collect and review interim data. They ensure the correct data are being collected and analyzed and then publish an annual progress

report. When reviewing the data, the committee recommends mid-course adjustments. Some of the measures that they have added to bring more breadth and depth to the balanced scorecard include:

- Attendance at student-parent-teacher conferences
- Elementary retentions
- Middle school retentions
- Graduation rate
- On-time bus delivery
- Preventable accidents per 100,000 miles traveled
- New teachers with the system after three years
- Variance of system budget to actual expenses
- Audit status
- Student perception of safety
- Staff perception of safety

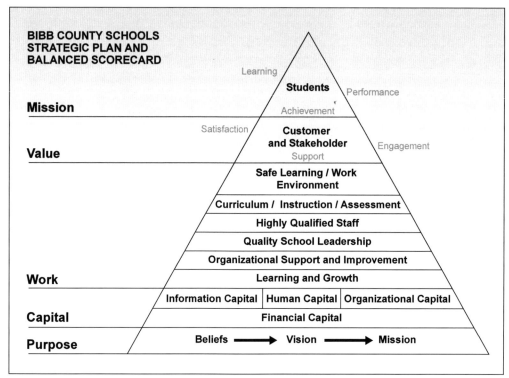

Thanks to Bibb County School District, Macon, Georgia.

In one rapidly growing district, both teacher and principal evaluation processes were redesigned to align with ongoing professional learning priorities. Teachers were invited to partner with other educators in deep learning around one of the district's priority growth areas. They established growth goals, collected evidence, and shared proof with the principal and others throughout the year. Principals were asked to follow a similar process of goal setting and evidence collection to be presented at mid-year and end-of-year conferences with central office leadership.

A district superintendent and assistant superintendent worked with principals and assistant principals from all district schools to craft a plan for using common, open-ended tasks as part of the overall assessment plan. The group discussed the added value of having the results from these tasks across the school year serve as feedback to the district about progress of students on targeted standards. They brainstormed possibilities for each of the core content areas. Leaders and teachers developed prompts and common scoring guides or criteria. For example, in mathematics, students periodically responded to one problem-solving task. Teachers gathered and collaboratively scored the papers, discussing next steps for teaching. The results were used to inform the district of the assessment *for* learning initiative, as well as informing teachers about their work with students.

Teachers and principals brainstormed a list of assessment *for* learning behaviors and practices they expected to see in a classroom. It became a checklist to be used by observers (principals and others) to give feedback. At the next faculty meeting, observers shared aloud some of what they had observed. Discussions then centered around what was working, what needed to be improved, and next steps. Over time, classroom teachers posted signs prior to the observations that alerted others: "As you walk through this classroom, please notice . . ." and "As you leave, record two compliments and a question."

One district leadership team worked hard to provide school board members with the "real news" of their assessment *for* learning initiative, over the course of several years. Instead of waiting until the end of each year to share information and data, they provided evidence of learning along the way—on a bimonthly basis. Besides sharing these smaller yet just-in-time pictures into the work that the schools, students, and educators were engaged in, the leadership team helped the board members to understand that this immediate evidence was as important and necessary as lengthy and comprehensive year-end reports. They framed the conversation around leading and lagging indicators. The power of leading indicators was to communicate that the status and the growth of the initiative were "right now." It was possible with this information to shift and adjust to emerging needs. If they waited until the close of the year and only shared lagging indicators, or that data that came at the end of the learning, not only would the excitement and the momentum have been missed along the way, but opportunities to react and plan for any adjustments would have been impossible.

One fast-growing district with rapidly changing demographics created a process for combining data from both standardized and classroom assessments. To help individual students in danger of not being promoted to the next grade level, a template for capturing and synthesizing data points was created. A team, consisting of the principal, classroom teacher, parents, and other personnel, met to develop an instructional plan for supporting the students. Included in the plan were teaching targets, agreed-upon evidence to be collected, and review dates every three months. Discussions and data from the evidence collected were used to plan next steps.

One district established School Assessment Leadership Teams to guide the learning of a complex of schools (five elementary, three middle, and two secondary schools). During this multiyear project, a representative group of teachers and administrators from each school met three times a year. The first two meetings of each year consisted of working with an external presenter/facilitator for two days. Each session involved deepening the leadership teams' knowledge of assessment, as well as providing them with practical strategies to support the learning of their colleagues. At the end of each session, the leadership team recorded what they were going to accomplish prior to the next gathering and shared their plan with colleagues from other schools. During the sessions, presentations, conversations, and in-depth interviews were recorded to document and support the work. This digital record, in addition to student achievement data, became evidence of the group's learning for everyone directly involved in the initiative, as well as the superintendent and the leadership team.

One school district has a district parent advisory council that includes two representatives from the parent council from each school. These representatives give feedback about different aspects of the education system. Periodically, they are asked to give feedback about assessment *for* learning and the reporting process.

One school, when revamping the student reporting process, engaged students and groups of parents in reviewing actual student reports (student and teacher names removed). Students and parents were surveyed anonymously about their experience with the reporting process. They made suggestions that were considered by the parent focus group and the student leadership team. Everyone had an opportunity to provide feedback to the teaching staff and leadership team regarding what was effective and what was not. The feedback was used to adjust the reporting process. After the second set of reports had gone home, students and parents were again invited to provide feedback. Surveys and focus groups continued during the first three years of the new reporting process.

One educational system uses a computer-based program that helps teachers construct classroom tests related to those portions of the curriculum that can be assessed by a test. Teachers select the test items, students take the test, teachers input the results, and then, the computer-based system provides comparison data. For example, a teacher can compare student results with similar-aged students in schools of comparable populations and socioeconomic status. These data help teachers and schools get past the barrier often expressed as, "Oh well, it's the best *our* students can do, given their learning needs."

"Feedback is among the most critical influences on student learning."

John Hattie and Helen Timperley

Lessons Learned

- Relying only on data that are easy to collect, such as summative data, is not good enough. Summative or lagging data, by their very nature, come at the end of the process—too late to provide feedback so that necessary adjustments can be made throughout the learning time.

- Identify information and data checkpoints that provide feedback during the process while there is still time to revise actions. Provide professional learning support, as needed, in response to ongoing data collecting.

- Consider using existing data points to inform an evaluation plan or decision making. In some instances, data can serve multiple purposes and can be mined from established databases.

- Create a plan. Outline the data and evidence to be collected and how they will be used in evaluating progress and in determining next steps. (See figure on facing page.)

Keeping on track requires that we celebrate our successes and be informed about what needs to be adjusted or changed. Valuable input and the involvement of others fuel our work. Effective leaders involve everyone in providing feedback to self, peers, and the system. Quality feedback that supports ongoing learning must be a continuous process rather than an event that occurs periodically.

Plan for Using Data

Guiding Questions	Consider . . .	Your Notes
What is our goal/target? What data could we collect in order to provide proof of reaching the stated goal/target?	-Data from differentiated sources -Student assessment data that include a broad range of sources -School-based data -District-based data	
Who will collect the data?	-External support -Internal support	
When will the data be collected?	-Monthly -Three times per year -Once per year	
How will the data be collected?	-Electronically -District-generated forms -Sent in by each school	
Who will collate the data? How?	-Committee -Individual -External support -Internal support	
Who will analyze the data?	-Committee -Superintendent's department -Board of trustees	
How will the findings be reported?	-Formal report -Executive summary -Brochure	
To whom will the findings be reported?	-System personnel -Community -Selected group	
When will the findings be reported?	-Yearly -Twice a year -Quarterly	

An outline of this figure can be found as a reproducible on page 157 of appendix 2.

As you reflect on the contents of this chapter, consider how essential questions can guide your work as leaders and how you can arrange to use the feedback to feed-forward the learning of the entire system and those within it. Use the guiding questions on the template (found on page 157 of appendix 2) to assist you in your planning around data collection and analysis.

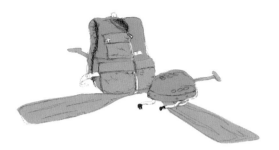

Standards-Based Reporting

Chapter 12

" Absence of evidence is not evidence of absence. "

Carl Sagan

The way we value and judge student achievement is changing. Standards-based curriculum, assessment, and instruction require us to change our grading and reporting practices. Assessment *for* learning is yet another reason to reconsider and redefine the way we measure success and report to others. How can we move forward in a way that captures what we know to be true about learning?

Standards-Based Reporting

A move to standards-based instruction requires a complementary move to standards-based reporting. Standards-based reporting is an example of assessment *of* learning. It is when teachers review the evidence of learning and make a professional judgment—an evaluation. Historically, teachers have struggled to ensure report card grades fairly reflect student learning and achievement. There are many issues related to traditional evaluation and grading practices.

Common evaluation practices such as grading in isolation, averaging marks and scores, limiting evidence to products such as tests to produce marks and grades for report cards, and using electronic grading programs on default settings cannot continue. There is a danger of misrepresenting student learning and achievement, especially for students who face the greatest challenges as they learn and are punished most by these reporting practices.

Systems of grading and reporting can be difficult to change, despite their inconsistencies, disparities, and poor quality. Yet educators who seek to improve classroom assessment in order that it better support learning must also take thoughtful steps to improve the quality of reporting. The job of reporting in a standards-based system is to report on learning and achievement—the *results* of work habits, personal responsibility, and learning. Furthermore, limiting evidence of learning to only grades and marks from tests and quizzes that take place throughout the course may unfairly penalize those students who need the fully allocated course time in order to learn. As we work toward standards-based reporting, we move cautiously. We include students, parents, and our colleagues in the conversations.

As we change grading and reporting practices, we look for everyday examples to illustrate the difficulties traditional grading practices pose. For example, consider how evaluation happens outside of the classroom or school. When we are working in a job, our performance is assessed in different ways—more aligned with the effort we make to improve our productivity and to get along well with others. As adults, we aren't repeatedly asked to take tests in order to maintain or advance our position. Imagine the consequences if a surgeon seeking a credential for a new procedure simply had to pass a written test to earn it. Consider the consequences in football if, after listening to the coach explain the desired maneuver, a defensive lineman was only required to respond, "Got it, Coach!" rather than demonstrate he could perform it.

Think about the process involved in getting a driver's license. Driver competency requires more than a simple test. A person seeking a driver's license takes a written test, but also drives in front of a witness (observation of process) and responds to questions about the decisions she or he makes (conversation). The information that informs the professional judgment comes from three sources; it is triangulated. The same logic applies to assessing and evaluating today's learning standards.

Testing–Grading–Retention Connections:

Lorrie A. Shepard's research focus includes evaluating test use, grade retention, teacher testing, effects of high-stakes testing, and classroom assessment. Her studies on the effects of retention and its relationship to the dropout rate found that students who repeated were 20 to 30 percent more likely to drop out of school.

The Truth About Learning

Reporting must capture and communicate truth about learning. To do so, it must be based on rich evidence of learning from multiple sources, exist as part of a communication and feedback-rich process that supports and enables the learner, and be understood by all audiences—students, parents, and other educators.

It is important to first envision what grading and reporting could look like if they reflected the desired principles of learning. How would assessment *for* learning practices help create a standards-based grading system that communicates truth about learning? Consider the following essential questions that can help you to check for alignment and consistency as you consider the reporting structures in your jurisdiction.

Essential Reporting Questions: Checking for Alignment and Consistency

The Learning Destination in Relation to Standards or Outcomes

1. Are report card grades given for the full range of educational standards or outcomes, not just those easiest to measure?

2. Has evidence of learning been selected because of its alignment with outcomes and standards?

Reliable and Valid Evidence of Learning

3. Are the report card grades based upon a wide array of evidence from multiple sources over time so as to ensure validity and reliability?

4. Do students understand expectations and acceptable evidence?

5. Are students involved in co-constructing criteria in relation to products, processes, and collections of evidence of learning?

6. Does the summative evaluation take place after students have time and opportunity to learn?

Evaluation at the End of Learning in Preparation for Reporting

7. Are report card grades derived from evidence present, not absent (thus devoid of practices such as assigning zeroes, grading on a curve, averaging, or penalty deductions)?

8. Are report card grades for achievement of standards or learning outcomes reported separately from other non-achievement factors such as effort, attitude, attendance, and punctuality?

9. Are report card grades reflective of a student's most consistent, more recent pattern of performance in relation to course learning goals based on the relevant standards and outcomes, as well as predetermined levels of quality?

Informed Professional Judgment

10. Do report card grades reflect informed teacher professional judgment of the level of quality of student work in relation to the standards or outcomes?

11. Are report card grades validated by and anchored in collaborative conversation and analysis of student work against agreed-upon criteria by teachers across grade levels and subjects?

12. Are report card grades reflective of and illustrated by collections of exemplars and samples that illustrate levels of quality and achievement?

Transforming traditional grading or marking practices means redefining the way we measure and report success to others. It requires shifting the beliefs of the school community and revising policies and practices so that judgments of learning will better communicate that which we choose to value. Here are some powerful examples from others who have begun this journey:

> After several years of work with teacher teams in assessment *for* learning and standards-based design, one large, rapidly growing urban school district decided to initiate a standards-based grading initiative. Initial work approved by the school board included framing district beliefs about assessment, learning, and grading. Teacher volunteers worked with internal and external consultants to design

and implement a standards-based report card. A communication campaign including parent forums, newsletters, and school meetings was begun. The district used ongoing feedback to design and implement standards-based report cards and focused professional development on assessment, grading, and reporting for all schools.

A small rural school district (K–12) initiated its work by involving many teachers and administrative leaders in identifying beliefs about assessment, evaluation, and grading, as well as practices and policies within their schools that conflicted with these beliefs. These conflicts were then sorted into short-term and long-term solution lists. Short-term conflicts were those deemed by the group as "non-negotiables," and changes in procedure and policy were made immediately to address them (i.e., no punitive grades for compliance issues like writing in ink or not placing name and date on papers). Long-term issues (i.e., non-academic report card categories, policy on zeroes, and make-up work) were examined at length by the group, and solutions found over the next six months of discussion were implemented over time with concurrent professional development. Standards-based report cards were implemented in one to two content areas at a time, across all levels of school (elementary, middle, and high) beginning with language arts and science.

One elementary school analyzed what was working and what was not working in regard to their reporting process. They focused on the effectiveness of current communication of student learning to the parent community. After research and presentations by resource people, they implemented a narrative report card based on information arising from student-parent-teacher conferences (see figure on page 106).

ELEMENTARY SCHOOL
SCHOOL DISTRICT # ___ (___)
PRIMARY PROGRESS REPORT

> **Student: D**
> **Reporting Period: November to March**
> **Teacher: Grade: 2**

This report describes your child's progress in relation to the curriculum in intellectual, social, human, and career development.

Introduction
____ is always ready to discover new things about his world and share his experiences with others. He contributes to a caring learning environment through the insightful questions he poses as he shares. His ideas reflect knowledge of the scientific inquiry process and bring new perspectives for us all to explore. He precipitates a synergistic caring learning environment through his enthusiasm to learn, generation of creative ideas and positive, specific feedback when listening to the contributions of others. As a result of his hard work, he has also successfully achieved the following goals from last term:
- To compute his math facts in his head to improve speed
- To develop more independence in developing storylines involving a beginning, middle, and end
- To independently apply learned spelling patterns when drafting his written ideas, especially usage of capital letters, punctuation, and verb endings like *ed* and *ing*
- To appreciate his strengths and celebrate his successes more often

Strengths/Accomplishments
- He reads age-appropriate texts using a variety of strategies including picture clues, blending, framing, skip reading, and predicting.
- He has developed an adequate sight word bank of personal and functional words.
- He can identify the main elements of a story including the title, author, illustrator, characters, main events, problem, and solution.
- He understands what he reads, can make judgements about the characters, and gives supporting evidence for his thinking.
- He uses library skills to research a topic and write key words to describe the appearance of a dinosaur.
- His personal spelling reflects a progressive knowledge of consonant sounds, short vowels, blends, some long vowel words with silent *e*, some words with vowel partners, and familiar words.
- He reads silently for progressively longer periods of time.
- He reads for a purpose, to pursue his interests, for pleasure, to sort and locate information, and find proof to support his thinking.
- He participated in the readers' theatre *Three Billy Goats Gruff* and publicly performed it with classmates.
- He is beginning to include more details in his storylines.
- He can add and subtract numbers to 20 with reasonable speed and accuracy.
- He can give the place value of numbers to 999 in terms of hundreds, tens, and ones and expanded notation (4 hundreds, 7 tens, and 9 ones = 400 + 70 + 9 = 479).
- He is learning to add with regrouping using an algorithm (278 + 106).
- He can independently skip count using more complex number patterns (by hundreds: 341, 441, 541).
- He generates creative and original ideas when imagining or developing expressions in the visual arts.
- He participates enthusiastically in partner activities.
- He is developing dancing, skating, and fitness skills to enhance endurance and balance.

Areas Requiring Further Attention or Development
I have no concerns regarding ____'s academic and personal development at this time.

Goals and Support for Learning
Goals:
- To apply the spelling patterns he has learned in his daily writing
- To further develop his written storylines to involve a beginning, middle, and end
- To ask questions to clarify meaning of difficult, unusual, or obscure words or ideas to improve comprehension

Support for learning:
Teacher will provide ____ with a graphic organizer to ensure all the elements of his storyline are considered before he writes and underline verb endings, plurals, and spelling patterns in his writing to edit.
____ is encouraged to:
- plan the characters, setting, problem and how the problem will be resolved before he writes
- watch for the beginning, middle, and end in the storylines of books he reads or videos he views

His parents might continue to read to/with ____ and explore ways his favorite authors extend story ideas and help him with his home spelling book.

Summary
____ is making satisfactory progress in all areas of his academic and personal development. He currently meets the widely held expectations for his age and minimally meets expectations in writing development. His cheerful optimism and eagerness to learn have motivated him to challenge himself, set realistic goals, develop a reasonable action plan, and persevere to completion. He is to be commended on his accomplishments. Congratulations on a job well done, ____!

Teacher _____   Principal _____

As part of a standards-based reporting initiative, one school leadership team decided to work with all teachers on faculty to prepare descriptions for each report card symbol (e.g.,1, 2, 3, 4 or ME, MP, N, U) that reflected the actual learning standards. These descriptions were used to give students and their parents a clear picture of the learning that was expected (see figure below).

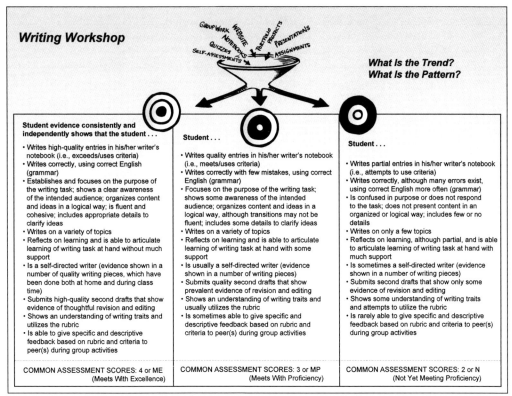

With thanks to Cresta McIntosh - Ma'ema'e Elementary, Hawaii for this example.

This figure can be found as a reproducible on page 158 of appendix 2.

In a time of drastic change it is the learners who inherit the future. The learned usually find themselves equipped to live in a world that no longer exists.

Eric Hoffer

Here is what people are trying as they work towards transforming traditional grading and reporting practices:

- Score student work collaboratively against agreed-upon criteria. The power of collaborative scoring should not be underestimated. It helps teachers internalize what quality looks like and to arrive at more consistent professional judgments.

- Gather and use metaphors and analogies from life outside of the classroom and school in order to move your learners to a deeper understanding of the purpose and complexity of reporting. Like the driver's license story from earlier in this chapter, this strategy helps both teachers and community members to come to recognize that intelligence, progress, and achievement cannot be neatly or simply communicated by one single grade or mark.

- Consider the full range of evidence (written, observed, conversational, constructed, and selected response) when making judgments of learning. Validity and reliability in classroom assessment arise from evidence of learning collected from multiple sources over time. Teachers require a plan to capture diverse evidence (see figure on page 110).

- Determine grades in relation to agreed-upon criteria and levels of quality rather than upon the numerical averages. Teacher judgment must be based on all the evidence of learning (qualitative and quantitative).

- Provide samples of quality performance tasks and scoring rubrics that teachers can access and use as models.

- Involve learners in using feedback and self-assessment against criteria throughout the learning process.

- Learn ways to change the settings on electronic grading programs so they more accurately represent student learning over time (rather than operating on default).

- Provide teachers with a continuum of professional learning opportunities that support their learning in this area.

- Create an ongoing and continuous communication plan. Report cards cannot be the only form of communication between home and school. Newsletters, daily or weekly emails, or blog posts are just some examples of ways to let parents know what students are learning.

- Consider carefully the timing and the process you would use to change or revise the report card at the district level. For some, a new report card can enhance classroom assessment practice. It can serve as a catalyst to involve students in understanding quality, in providing specific and descriptive feedback to self and others, and in collecting and communicating evidence of their learning. Yet, the process of creating or implementing a new report card can become a singular focus that drains some of their energy and initiative. The dialogue and debate overshadow conversations of effective classroom pedagogy. The broader goal of engaging students in their learning is lost in the rhetoric of opposing views and questions that seem to have few answers.

Learning Destination for Language Arts	Possible Evidence	My Evidence Includes
Reads and views a wide variety of materials in different genres	• Reader response notebook • List of books read and videos viewed • Completed genre web • Class work • Discussions • Informal conferences • Demonstrations • Observations of home reading	– My reader response notebook – My list of books read and videos viewed – My completed genre web
Writes/represents responses that show an understanding of what they have read	• Reader response notebook • Selected best response • Self-assessment • Observations from peers and others • Class work and discussions • Informal conference	– My top three best responses – Two self-assessments from this term – Dialogue journal with entries from Rahim and Jamile marked
Writes on or represents a range of topics in different forms for a variety of audiences	• Writing portfolio • List of topics written about • Collection of storyboards • Writing/representing forms checklist • Class work • Discussions • Informal conferences • Demonstrations	– My writing portfolio – The list of topics I focused on this term – Storyboards for my iMovie – Checklist of genres
Shows an understanding of the rules and conventions of writing	• Class work • Final publications • Writing/representing portfolio • Editing samples • Test scores	– Test scores – Three sets of first drafts from my portfolio
Works successfully on their own and in groups	• Peer assessments (using rubric) • Self-assessment (using rubric) • Group project results • Individual assignment marks	– A rubric from my iMovie group – Three top individual assignments
As you look at my evidence, please notice . . .	that I have really improved since the beginning. I think my work is of good quality.	

Adapted from *Conferencing and Reporting* by Gregory, Cameron, and Davies, 2011.

An outline of this figure can be found as a reproducible on page 159 of appendix 2.

We must create a reporting process that communicates clearly and accurately while supporting continued student learning. It is a necessary ingredient if assessment *for* learning is going to make a difference for student learning and achievement. At this point in North America there is evidence that educators are working with students and parents to transform grading practices. The work is not yet complete. Our advice? Move forward relentlessly and cautiously, involving everyone in the conversation along the way.

There are four key challenges that, as leaders, we need to consider as we shift to standards-based reporting:

1. Ensuring the evaluation process is standards-based

2. Ensuring there is a similar understanding of what quality looks like (remember the discussion about using samples or exemplars)

3 Ensuring the findings are reliable and valid

4. Involving parents, students, and all colleagues in the work of transforming traditional grading practices

---

Assessment Criteria–Learning Connections:

Royce Sadler's work focuses on assessing student learning, grading, assessment policy and practice, and improving university teaching. His article titled "Formative Assessment and the Design of Instructional Systems" (1989) articulates the reasons why clear criteria are necessary if students are to learn and serves as a foundation for subsequent work in formative assessment.

As leaders we can inadvertently create a significant barrier to achieving the promise of assessment *for* learning in classrooms when we neglect to move forward in our work of transforming traditional grading practices. We wish we could give you "the answer" for your system. We can't. Your jurisdiction's next answer to this significant challenge will emerge from your work with students, teachers, and parents. And, as we learn more and technology advances, that answer will keep changing. That is our work. We do know, however, that as you apply the ideas in this book you will chart your own system's path forward to a reporting process that communicates student learning in relation to standards, more clearly, more fairly, and more truthfully.

Activity: Evaluation—Exploring Letter Grades

Arrange to have one or two plates with something good to eat wrapped tightly with clear plastic (e.g., candies, cookies, different squares) available for this activity. It is important to note that each plate needs to contain five different kinds of items and hold enough so everyone in the room can have at least one to eat when the activity is finished. For example, each plate contains two Tootsie Rolls, two mini chocolate bars, two packages of licorice, two individually wrapped toffees, and two mini Rice Krispie squares. Participants are asked to look but not touch.

This activity is done in three stages.

Step 1. Ask participants to make a judgment and give each kind of item a letter grade (A, B, C) without talking or without showing others what they have done. This is an individual activity only.

Step 2. When finished, ask participants to work with their group and, through discussion, come to agreement and assign letter grades to each item. No voting or intimidation. Group members need to reach consensus after dialogue.

Step 3. When the groups are finished, ask them to number off and form into new groups and become a representative of their group. Their task is to come to agreement again around their previous evaluation in their new group.

This figure can be found as a reproducible on page 160 of appendix 2.

Task 1:
Reflect on your current practices. What do grading and reporting look like? How have they changed since you joined the profession? Do the policies require that reports focus on attainment of standards or learning outcomes? Is there a requirement to consider both qualitative and quantitative evidence, or are numerical data currently sufficient? How are classroom teachers informing their professional judgments with regard to appropriate quality levels? What is the role of technology? Is it being used to demand more marking and summative evaluation, or is it being used to show evidence of learning—proof of learning—over time? How involved are students and parents in the reporting process?

Task 2:
With your leadership team colleagues take about 30–60 minutes (depending on the size of the group) to conduct the activity titled Evaluation—Exploring Letter Grades (see figure on page 112). When you are finished, record your reflection.

This activity, by design, tends to fall apart during stage three as each participant uses unstated personal criteria for making judgments. When chaos has begun to reign and participants have struggled enough, call them back to order and invite them to consider what it was about the process that created the chaos. Why was it difficult to make judgments about assigning letter grades? Ask them to record their thoughts about implications for assigning grades at report card time. Invite participants to share their insights. Some of the points participants make often include:

- You need criteria before you begin evaluating.

- You need to communicate it clearly.

- The purpose or goal needs to be clear.

- The audience receiving the evaluative information must be clearly defined.

- Without criteria, personal preferences become the unstated criteria. At this point, the professional judgments—evaluations—are not standards-based.

- All assessment and evaluation are subjective. What is important is that you establish clear criteria in relation to standards and have enough evidence to ensure your findings are reliable and valid.

Note that evaluating and reporting are assessment *of* learning activities; the evaluator reviews the triangulated evidence of learning gathered in relation to the learning destination. As evaluators consider this learning destination (based on the standards), they ask themselves if the evidence shows that the person being evaluated has learned what needed to be learned to the appropriate degree of quality.

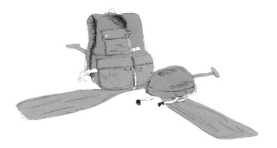

Final Thoughts

"Smooth seas do not make skillful sailors."

African proverb

The work of change can be exhausting. Though we know that it is essential and the challenges are inevitable, we may feel our inner resources are depleted and our energy levels are low. We need to build in time to rejuvenate. The way we do this varies for each of us; it may mean attending a professional learning event, visiting schools and classrooms, or regularly scheduling breakfast meetings with valued colleagues, as well as making time for yourself, for your family, and for fitness. Whatever it takes, we must purposefully plan for it. This vital time is when energy is renewed and resilience is created. This is how we build the sturdy foundation that gives us confidence in ourselves and our team. This is what equips us to take the next necessary steps and to prepare ourselves for the journey through change.

Leading change requires courage. We must consciously and deliberately work through it with grace, honesty, and humor. We do that together with our colleagues, as a team. As leaders, we must acknowledge that we will make mistakes. We must actively seek solutions, while modeling how assessment *for* learning supports and guides our daily work.

Learning–Intelligence Connections:

Robert Sternberg views intelligence as modifiable rather than fixed. Research suggests that successful people achieve success by identifying and capitalizing on their strengths, and identifying and correcting or compensating for their weaknesses. His theory is called "practical intelligence."

Focusing a system on assessment *for* learning is the key to improving learning for everyone. Both our intuition and the research confirm this. As leaders, it is important that we spend time reading about assessment *for* learning, speaking to our colleagues about their initiatives, and observing teachers in action. In other words, we are engaged in pre-contemplation, contemplation, and initiation (Davies et al. 2004). This precedes action. Then, as we survey our surroundings—staff, provincial/state directions, other districts, political climate, community—the window of opportunity will present itself.

Assessment–Motivation for Learning Connections:

Richard J. Stiggins' research on teachers' day-to-day assessment decisions and the time given to informally assessing learning in the midst of instruction formed the foundation for attention to classroom assessment and educators' assessment literacy. His work continues to reveal powerful connections between learners' assessment experience and their motivation to learn. He says if we wish to maximize student achievement in the US, we must pay far greater attention to the improvement of classroom assessment. Both assessment *for* learning and assessment *of* learning are essential.

Although we may have built readiness, developed initial capacity, and spent time foreshadowing, we know that the path ahead will not necessarily be smooth. It helps to see these challenges as "leadable" moments for us and our colleagues. Making it through the rapids together builds team spirit. Each stage of the journey is cause for celebration.

Leadership Connections:

Terrence Deal and Lee Bolman have co-authored a number of books on leadership and organizations. They argue that effective leadership resides in the soul, faith, and powerful habits of mind. Further, when we examine our work from different perspectives or frames, we are more able to find powerful solutions.

Transforming Schools and Systems Using Assessment: A Practical Guide has gathered success stories from our work and from other leaders to help inform your possible action. As you think about what you have read, you have identified patterns and themes. You have developed an internal list of what might work in your context and what would need to be adapted. As you worked through the leadership team activities, you extended your repertoire and engaged in conversation. Effective leaders observe, learn from, and reflect with others. They measure others' experiences against their own, and they construct and adjust understanding, alone and together. Then they are able to draw on these personal resources as they transform schools and systems with positive energy and optimism.

The companion book in this leadership series is titled *Leading the Way to Assessment* for *Learning: A Practical Guide*. It illustrates what assessment *for* learning looks like at the classroom, school, and district levels and how leaders can support teachers and colleagues in their practice. We hope it can also serve as a useful guide for you on your journey to successful learning for all.

"Everything changed the day he figured out there was exactly enough time for the important things in his life."

Brian Andreas

Acknowledgments

"We cannot hold a torch to light another's path without brightening our own."

Ben Sweetland

As we wrote this book, we referred to the many fine educational researchers and writers whose work informs, challenges, and guides us. Alongside these experts, we also acknowledge practitioners—students, teachers, administrators, district personnel, and community members. Thank you for allowing us to walk beside you. Through conversation, observation, and collaboration we have come to a better understanding of ourselves and the world around us. You have all been powerful teachers.

Anne, Sandra, and Beth

References and Resources

Allexsaht-Snider, M. 1995. Teachers' perspectives on their work with families in a bilingual community. *Research in Childhood Education*, 9, no. 2: 85–95.

Anthony, R., Johnson, T., Mickelson, N., and Preece, A. 1991. *Evaluating Literacy: A Perspective for Change*. Portsmouth, NH: Heinemann.

Aronson, E. 1972. *The Social Animal*. New York: Viking.

Assessment Reform Group (ARG). 2006. *The Role of Teachers in the Assessment of Learning*. Pamphlet produced by Assessment Systems for the Future project (ASF), Assessment Reform Group, UK.

Barth, R. 2004. *Learning by Heart*. Hoboken, NJ: Wiley.

Berger, P. and Luckmann, T. 1966. *The Social Construction of Reality: A Treatise in the Sociology of Knowledge*. Garden City, NY: Anchor Books.

Berliner, D. and Biddle, B. 1997. *The Manufactured Crisis: Myths, Frauds and the Attack on America's Public Schools*. New York: Longman.

Black, P. and Wiliam, D. 1998. Assessment and classroom learning. *Assessment in Education* 5, no. 1: 7–75.

Bolman, L. and Deal, T. 2008. *Reframing Organizations: Artistry, Choice and Leadership*, 4th Edition. San Francisco: Jossey-Bass.

Boud, D. 1995. *Enhancing Learning Through Self Assessment*. London: Kogan Page.

Brice Heath, S. 1983. *Ways With Words: Language, Life and Work in Communities and Classrooms*. Cambridge, MA: Cambridge University Press.

Brookhart, S. 2001. Students' formative and summative uses of assessment information. *Assessment in Education* 8, no. 21: 153–169.

Brookhart, S. 2003. Developing measurement theory for classroom assessment purposes and uses. *Educational Measurement: Issues and Practice* 22, no. 4: 5–12.

Brooks, J. and Brooks, M. 1993. *In Search of Understanding: The Case for Constructivist Classrooms.* Alexandria, VA: Association for Supervision and Curriculum Development.

Bruner, J. 1960. *The Process of Education.* Cambridge, MA: Harvard University Press.

Bruner, J. 1966. *Toward a Theory of Instruction.* Cambridge, MA: Belknap Press.

Bruner, J. 1978. The role of dialogue in language acquisition. In A. Sinclair, R. J. Jarvelle, and W. J. M. Levelt (Eds.), *The Child's Concept of Language.* New York: Springer-Verlag.

Bruner, J. 1986. *Actual Minds, Possible Worlds.* Cambridge, MA: Harvard University Press.

Bruner, J. 1996. *The Culture of Education.* Cambridge, MA: Harvard University Press.

Burns, M. 1995. *Writing in Math Class: A Resource for Grades 2–8.* Sausalito, CA: Math Solutions.

Butler, R. 1987. Task-involving and ego-involving properties of evaluation: Effects of different feedback conditions on motivational perceptions, interest and performance. *Journal of Educational Psychology* 79, no. 4: 474–482.

Butler, R. 1988. Enhancing and undermining intrinsic motivation: The effects of task-involving and ego-involving evaluation on interest and performance. *British Journal of Educational Psychology* 58: 1–14.

Butler, R. and Nisan, M. 1986. Effects of no feedback, task-related comments and grades on intrinsic motivation and performance. *Journal of Educational Psychology* 78, no. 3: 210–216.

Butterworth, R. W. and Michael, W. B. 1975. The relationship of reading achievement, school attitude, and self-responsibility behaviors of sixth grade pupils to comparative and individuated reporting systems: Implication of improvement of validity of the evaluation and pupil performance. *Educational and Psychological Measurement* 35: 987–991.

Caine, R. N. and Caine, G. 1991. *Making Connections: Teaching and the Human Brain*. Alexandria, VA: Association for Supervision and Curriculum Development.

Caine, R. N. and Caine, G. 1997. *Education on the Edge of Possibility*. Alexandria, VA: Association for Supervision and Curriculum Development.

Calkins, L. 1991. *Living Between the Lines*. Portsmouth, NH: Heinemann.

Cantalini, M. 1987. *The Effects of Age and Gender on School Readiness and School Success*. Unpublished doctoral dissertation. Toronto: Ontario Institute for Studies in Education.

Carr, W. and Kemmis, S. 1986. *Becoming Critical: Education, Knowledge, and Action Research*. London: Falmer Press.

Ceci, S. J. 1990. *On Intelligence—More or Less: A Bio-Ecological Treatise on Intellectual Development*. Englewood Cliffs, NJ: Prentice Hall.

Champion, R. 2004. Taking measure: 10 questions to help reshape the professional development calendar. *Journal of Staff Development* 25, no. 4: 61–62.

Cicourel, A., Jennings, K. W., Jennings, S. H. M., Leiter, K. C. W., MacKay, R., Mehan, H., and Roth, D. R. (Eds.). 1974. *Language Use and School Performance*. New York: Academic Press.

Clay, M. 1993. *Reading Recovery: A Guidebook for Teachers in Training*. Portsmouth, NH: Heinemann.

Colvin, G. 2008. *Talent Is Overrated: What Really Separates World-Class Performers From Everybody Else*. New York: Penguin.

Costa, A. L. and Garmston, R. J. 1994. *Cognitive Coaching: A Foundation for Renaissance Schools*. Norwood, MA: Christopher-Gordon.

Covington, M. V. 1998. *The Will to Learn: A Guide for Motivating Young People*. New York: Cambridge University Press.

Crooks, T. 1988. The impact of classroom evaluation practices on students. *Review of Educational Research* 58, no. 4: 438–481.

Curwin, R. 1978. The grades of wrath: Some alternatives. *Learning* 6, no. 6: 60–64.

Darling-Hammond, L., Chung Wei, R., Andree, A., Richardson, N., and Orphanos, S. 2009. *Professional Learning in the Learning*

Profession: A Status Report on Teacher Development in the United States and Abroad. Stanford, CA: National Staff Development Council.

Davies, A. 2004. *Finding Proof of Learning in a One-to-One Computing Classroom*. Courtenay, BC: Connections.

Davies, A., Arbuckle, M., and Bonneau, D. 2004. Assessment *for* learning: Planning for a professional development audience. *Online Journal: Research into Practice*. Retrieved November 23, 2011, from http://electronicportfolios.org/afl/Assessment4learning.pdf.

Davies, A., Cameron, C., Politano, C., and Gregory, K. 1992. *Together Is Better: Collaborative Assessment, Evaluation, and Reporting*. Winnipeg, MB: Peguis.

DeCharms, R. 1968. *Personal Causation*. New York: Academic Press.

DeCharms, R. 1972. Personal causation training in schools. *Journal of Applied Social Psychology* 2: 95–113.

Deci, E., and Ryan, R. M. 1985. *Intrinsic Motivation and Self-Determination in Human Behavior*. New York: Plenum Press.

Deci, E., and Ryan, R. M. 2002. *Handbook of Self-Determination Research*. New York: University of Rochester Press.

Delpit, L. 1995. *Other People's Children: Cultural Conflict in the Classroom*. New York: New Press.

Dewey, J. 1910. *How We Think*. Lexington, MA: D. C. Heath & Co.

Dewey, J. 1964. My pedagogic creed. In R. D. Archambault (Ed.), *John Dewey on Education: Selected Writings*. Chicago: University of Chicago Press.

De Geus, A. 2002. *The Living Company: Habits for Survival in a Turbulent Business Environment*. Watertown, MA: Harvard Business.

Dornbusch, S. 1994. School Tracking Harms Millions, Sociologist Finds. Stanford University News Service. Retrieved March 2, 1994, from www.stanford.edu/dept/news/pr/94/940302Arc4396.html.

DuFour, R., DuFour, R., Eaker, R., and Many, T. 2006. *Learning by Doing: A Handbook for Professional Learning Communities at Work*. Bloomington, IN: Solution Tree Press.

DuFour, R. and Eaker, R. 1998. *Professional Learning Communities at Work: Best Practices for Enhancing Student Achievement.* Bloomington, IN: National Educational Services.

Dweck, C. S. 2000. *Self-Theories: Their Role in Motivation, Personality, and Development.* Philadelphia: Psychology Press.

Dweck, C. S. and Leggett, E. L. 1988. A social-cognitive approach to motivation and personality. *Psychological Review* 95, no. 2: 256–273.

Elbow, P. 1986. *Embracing Contraries: Explorations in Learning and Teaching.* New York: Oxford University Press.

Ellis, J. 1968. *The Effects of Same Sex Class Organization of Junior High School Students' Academic Achievement, Self-Discipline, Self-Concept, Sex-Role Identification and Attitudes Toward School.* Washington, DC: US Department of Health, Education, and Welfare.

Epstein, J. 2010. *School, Family, and Community Partnerships: Preparing Educators and Improving Schools*, 2nd Edition. Boulder, CO: Westview Press.

Erickson, H. L. 1998. *Concept-Based Curriculum and Instruction: Teaching Beyond the Facts.* Thousand Oaks, CA: Corwin Press.

Farr, B. P. and Trumbull, E. 1997. *Assessment Alternatives for Diverse Classrooms.* Norwood, MA: Christopher-Gordon.

Feuerstein, R. 1990. The theory of structural cognitive modifiability. In B. Z. Presseisen (Ed.), *Learning and Thinking Styles: Classroom Interaction* (pp. 68–134). Washington, DC: National Education Association.

Fuchs, L. S. and Fuchs, D. A. 1985. *Quantitative Synthesis of Effects of Formative Evaluation of Achievement.* Paper presented at the annual meeting of the American Educational Research Association, Chicago. ERIC Doc. #ED256781.

Fullan, M. 2001. *Leading in a Culture of Change.* San Francisco: Jossey-Bass.

Fullan, M., Cuttress, C., and Kilcher, A. 2005. 8 forces for leaders of change. *Journal of Staff Development* 26, no. 4: 54–58, 64.

Funk, H. D. 1969. Nonpromotion teaches children they are inferior. *Education Digest* 35, no. 3: 38–39.

Gardner, J. (Ed.). 2006. *Assessment and Learning.* Thousand Oaks, CA: SAGE.

Garmston, R. J. 2005. Group wise: No time for learning? Just take it in tiny bites and savor it. *Journal of Staff Development* 26, no. 4.

Garmston, R. J. and Wellman, B. 2009. *The Adaptive School: A Sourcebook for Developing Collaborative Groups*, 2nd Edition. Norwood, MA: Christopher-Gordon.

Gazzaniga, M. 1992. *Nature's Mind: The Biological Roots of Thinking, Emotions, Sexuality, Language, and Intelligence*. New York: Basic Books.

Gladwell, M. 2008. *Outliers: The Story of Success*. New York: Little, Brown.

Goleman, D. 1996. *Emotional Intelligence: Why It Can Matter More Than IQ*. New York: Bantam Books.

Gould, S. J. 1981. *The Mismeasure of Man*. New York: Norton.

Gredler, G. R. 1984. Transition classes: A viable alternative to the at-risk child. *Psychology in the Schools* 21, no. 4: 463–470.

Gregory, K., Cameron, C., and Davies, A. 2011. *Conferencing and Reporting*, 2nd Edition. Bloomington, IN: Solution Tree Press.

Hargreaves, A. 2003. *Teaching in the Knowledge Society: Education in the Age of Insecurity*. New York: Teachers College Press.

Harlen, W. 2006. The role of assessment in developing motivation for learning. In J. Gardner (Ed.), *Assessment and Learning* (pp. 61–80). Thousand Oaks, CA: SAGE.

Harlen, W. and Deakin Crick, R. 2003. Testing and motivation for learning. *Assessment in Education* 10, no. 2: 169–208.

Harter, S. 1978. Pleasure derived from challenge and the effects of receiving grades on children's difficulty level choices. *Child Development* 49, no. 3: 788–799.

Hattie, J. 1992. Measuring the effects of schooling. *Australian Journal of Education* 36, no. 1: 5–13.

Hattie, J. and Timperley, H. 2007. The power of feedback. *Review of Educational Research* 77, no. 1: 81–112.

Healy, J. 1990. *Endangered Minds*. New York: Touchstone.

Hill, J., Reeves, T. C., Grant, M., Wang, S.-K., and Wan, S. 2002. *The Impact of Portable Technologies on Teaching and Learning*. Year Three Report. Paper presented at the annual meeting of the American Educational Research Association, New Orleans. Retrieved September 11, 2003, from http://lpsl.coe.uga.edu /projects/aalaptop/pdf/aa3rd/Year3ReportFinalVersion.pdf.

Holmes, C. T. 1989. Grade level retention effects: A meta-analysis of research studies. In L. A. Shepard and M. L. Smith (Eds.), *Flunking Grades: The Policies and Effects of Retention* (pp. 16–33). London: Falmer Press.

Holmes, C. T. and Matthews, K. M. 1984. The effects of nonpromotion on elementary and junior high school pupils: A meta-analysis. *Review of Educational Research* 54, no. 2: 225–236.

Holmes, C. T. and Saturday, J. 2000. Promoting the end of retention. *Journal of Curriculum and Supervision* 15, no. 4: 300–314.

James, M., Black, P., McCormick, R., Pedder, D., and Wiliam, D. 2006. Learning how to learn, in classrooms, schools and networks: Aims, design and analysis. *Research Papers in Education—Special Issue* 21, no. 2: 101–118.

James, M., McCormick, R., Black, P., Carmichael, P., Drummond, M. J., Fox, A., MacBeath, J., Marshall, B., Pedder, D., Procter, R., Swaffield, S., Swann, J., and Wiliam, D. 2007. *Improving Learning How to Learn—Classrooms, Schools and Networks*. London: Routledge.

Jensen, E. 1998. *Teaching With the Brain in Mind*. Alexandria, VA: Association for Supervision and Curriculum Development.

Jeroski, S. 2003. *Wireless Writing Project: School District No. 60 (Peace River North) Research Report: Phase II*. Vancouver, BC: Horizon Research & Evaluation.

Kamii, C. 1984. Autonomy: The aim of education envisioned by Piaget. *Phi Delta Kappan* 65, no. 6: 410–415.

Kilborn, B. 1990. *Constructive Feedback: Learning the Art*. Toronto: Ontario Institute for Studies in Education Press; Cambridge, MA: Brookline Books.

Kohn, A. 1993. *Punished by Rewards: The Trouble With Gold Stars, Incentive Plans, A's, Praise, and Other Bribes*. New York: Houghton Mifflin.

Kulik, J. A. and Kulik, L. C. 1992. Meta-analytic findings on grouping programs. *Gifted Child Quarterly* 36, no. 2: 73–77.

Kyle, J. 1992. *Literature Review: Letter Grades and Anecdotal Reporting*. Internal Working Document, Ministry of Education.

Langer, E. J. 1997. *The Power of Mindful Learning.* Reading, MA: Addison-Wesley.

Langer, J. and Applebee, A. 1986. Reading and writing instruction: Toward a theory of teaching and learning. *Review of Research in Education* 13: 171–194.

LeMahieu, P. G. 1996. From authentic assessment to authentic accountability. In J. Armstrong (Ed.), *Roadmap for Change: A Briefing for the Second Education Summit.* Denver, CO: Education Commission of the States.

Lepper, M. R. and Greene, D. 1974. Turning play into work: Effects of adult surveillance and extrinsic rewards on children's intrinsic motivation. *Journal of Personality and Social Psychology* 45, no. 4: 1141–1145.

Lewin, K. 1952. Group decision and social change. In G. E. Swanson, T. M. Newcomb, and E. L. Hartley (Eds.), *Readings in Social Psychology.* New York: Holt.

Lieberman, M. and Langer, E. J. 1995. Mindfulness in the process of learning. In E. J. Langer (Ed.), *The Power of Mindful Learning.* Reading, MA: Addison-Wesley.

Light, D., McDermott, M., and Honey, M. 2002. *The Impact of Ubiquitous Portable Technology on an Urban School-Project Hiller.* New York: Center for Children and Technology. Retrieved September 12, 2003, from www2.edc.org/CCT/admin/publications/report/Hiller-Final.pdf.

Lowther, D., Ross, S., and Morrison, G. 2001. *Evaluation of a Laptop Program: Successes and Recommendation.* Paper presented at the "Building on the Future" NECC 2001: National Educational Computing Conference Proceedings, Chicago, June 25–27, 2001. Retrieved September 11, 2003, from home.earthlink.net/~anebl/lowther.pdf.

Luria, A. R. 1981. *Language and Cognition.* New York: Wiley.

Macdonald, C. 1982. A better way of reporting. *BC Teacher* 61 (March/April): 142–144.

Maehr, M. 1974. *Sociocultural Origins of Achievement.* Monterey, CA: Brooks/Cole.

Mager, R. F. and McCann, J. 1963. *Learner Controlled Instruction.* Palo Alto, CA: Varian Press.

Mahoney, M. J. 1974. *Cognition and Behavior Modification*. Cambridge, MA: Ballinger.

Marzano, R. J. 2000. *Transforming Classroom Grading*. Alexandria, VA: Association for Supervision and Curriculum Development.

Marzano, R. J., Pickering, D. J., and Pollock, J. E. 2001. *Classroom Instruction That Works: Research-Based Strategies for Increasing Student Achievement*. Alexandria, VA: Association for Supervision and Curriculum Development.

Marzano, R. J., Waters, T., and McNulty, B. 2005. *School Leadership That Works: From Research to Results*. Alexandria, VA: Association for Supervision and Curriculum Development.

Mehan, H. 1973. Assessing children's language using abilities. In J. M. Armer and A. S. Grimshaw (Eds.), *Methodological Issues in Comparative Sociological Research* (pp. 309–343). New York: Wiley.

Mintzberg, H. 2004. *Managers, not MBAs: A Hard Look at the Soft Practice of Managing and Management Development*. San Francisco: Berrett-Koehler.

Natriello, G. 1984. Problems in the evaluation of students and student disengagement from secondary schools. *Journal of Research and Development in Education* 17, no. 4: 14–24.

Neilsen, L. 1994. *A Stone in My Shoe*. Winnipeg, MB: Peguis. Retrieved November 14, 2011, from http://umanitoba.ca/cm/vol2/no15/stone.html.

Newman, V. 1994. *Math Journals: Tools for Authentic Assessment*. San Leandro, CA: Teacher Resource Center.

Niklason, L. B. 1987. Do certain groups of children profit from a grade retention? *Psychology in the Schools* 24, no. 4: 339–345.

Oakes, J. 1985. *Keeping Track: How Schools Structure Inequality*. New Haven, CT: Yale University Press.

Overman, M. 1986. Student promotion and retention. *Phi Delta Kappan* 67, no. 8: 609–613.

Palincsar, A. S. and Brown, A. L. 1986. Interactive teaching to promote independent learning from text. *The Reading Teacher* 39, no. 8: 771–777.

Palmer Wolf, D., LeMahieu, P. G., and Eresh, J. 1992. Good measure: Assessment as a tool for educational reform. *Educational Leadership* 49, no. 8: 8–13.

Papert, S. 1980. *Mindstorms: Children, Computers, and Powerful Ideas.* New York: Basic Books.

Papert, S. 1999. *Diversity in Learning: A Vision for the New Millennium Parts 1 & 2,* Diversity Task Force convened by Vice President Al Gore.

Peters, T. 2005. *Leadership (Essentials).* New York: Dorling Kindersley.

Peters, T. and Waterman, R. 1982. *In Search of Excellence: Lessons From America's Best Run Companies.* New York: Harper & Row.

Peterson, S. E., DeGracie, J. S., and Ayabe, C. R. 1987. A longitudinal study of the effects of retention/promotion on academic achievement. *American Educational Research Journal* 24, no. 1: 107–118.

Phillips, D. C. 1995. The good, the bad, and the ugly: The many faces of constructivism. *Educational Researcher* 24, no. 7: 5–12.

Popham, W. J. 1993. Circumventing the high costs of authentic assessment. *Phi Delta Kappan* 74, no. 6: 470–473.

Preece, A. 1995. Involving students in self-evaluation. In A. Costa and B. Kallick (Eds.), *Assessment in the Learning Organization.* Alexandria, VA: Association for Supervision and Curriculum Development.

Preece, J. (Ed.). 1993. *A Guide to Usability. Human Factors in Computing.* Wokingham, UK: Addison-Wesley.

Prochaska, J., Norcross, J., and DiClemente, C. 1994. *Changing for Good: A Revolutionary Six-Stage Program for Overcoming Bad Habits and Moving Your Life Positively Forward.* New York: HarperCollins.

Purkey, W. and Novak, J. 1984. *Inviting School Success.* Belmont, CA: Wadsworth.

Reeves, D. (Ed.). 2007. *Ahead of the Curve: The Power of Assessment to Transform Teaching and Learning.* Bloomington, IN: Solution Tree Press.

Restak, R. 1988. *The Mind.* New York: Bantam Books.

Rock, D. 2009. *Your Brain at Work*. New York: HarperBusiness.

Rockman, S. 2003. Learning from laptops. In Cable in the Classroom's *Threshold Magazine 1*, no. 1: 24–28.

Rockman, S. et al. 2000. *A More Complex Picture: Laptop Use and Impact in the Context of Changing Home and School Access*. The third in a series of research studies on Microsoft's Anytime Anywhere Learning Program. Retrieved November 23, 2011, from www.rockman.com/projects/126.micro.aal/yr3_report.pdf.

Rosenthal, R., and Jacobson, L. 1992. *Pygmalion in the Classroom: Teacher Expectation and Pupils' Intellectual Development,* Expanded edition. New York: Irvington.

Rothman, R. 1995. *Measuring Up: Standards, Assessment and School Reform.* San Francisco: Jossey-Bass.

Rubin, H. 2001. The perfect vision of Dr. V. *Fast Company*. Issue 43. January 2001. Retrieved November 14, 2011, from www.fastcompany.com/magazine/43/drv.html.

Russell, M., Bebell, D., Cowan, J., and Corbelli, M. April 2002. *An AlphaSmart for Each Student: Does Teaching and Learning Change With Full Access to Word Processors?* Retrieved August 26, 2003, from www.bc.edu/research/intasc/PDF/AlphaSmartEachStudent.pdf.

Sadler, D. R. 1989. Formative assessment and the design of instructional systems. *Instructional Science* 16, no. 2: 119–144.

Schlechty, P. 2009. *Leading for Learning: How to Transform Schools into Learning Organizations.* San Francisco: Jossey-Bass.

Schön, D. A. 1983. *The Reflective Practitioner*. New York: Basic Books.

Schön, D. A. 1987. *Educating the Reflective Practitioner.* San Francisco: Jossey-Bass.

Schwartz, J. 1991. Let them assess their own learning. *The English Journal* 80, no. 2: 67–73.

Seagoe, M. V. 1970. *The Learning Process and School Practice*. Scranton, PA: Chandler.

Senge, P. 2006. *The Fifth Discipline: The Art and Practice of the Learning Organization,* 2nd Edition. New York: Crown.

Sergiovanni, T. 1994. *Building Communities in Schools*. San Francisco: Jossey-Bass.

Shepard, L. A. 1989. Why we need better assessments. *Educational Leadership*, 46, no. 7: 4–9.

Shepard, L. A. 2000. The role of assessment in a learning culture. *Educational Researcher* 29, no. 7: 4–14.

Shepard, L. A. and Smith, M. L. 1987. What doesn't work: Explaining policies of retention in the early grades. *Phi Delta Kappan* 69: 129–134.

Shepard, L. A. and Smith, M. L. 1989a. *Flunking Grades: Research and Policies on Retention.* New York: Falmer Press.

Shepard, L. A. and Smith, M. L. 1989b. Synthesis of research on school readiness and kindergarten retention. In R. S. Brandt (Ed.), *Readings on Research From Educational Leadership.* Alexandria, VA: Association for Supervision and Curriculum Development.

Slavin, R. E. 1987. Ability grouping and student achievement in elementary schools: A best-evidence synthesis. *Review of Educational Research* 57, no. 3: 293–336.

Slavin, R. E. 1990. Achievement effects of ability grouping in secondary schools: A best-evidence synthesis. *Review of Educational Research* 60, no. 3: 471–499.

Slavin, R. E. 1996. Research for the future: Research on cooperative learning and achievement: What we know, what we need to know. *Contemporary Educational Psychology* 21: 43–69.

Smith, F. 1986. *Insult to Intelligence: The Bureaucratic Invasion of Our Classrooms.* Portsmouth, NH: Heinemann.

Smith, F. 1995. *Between Hope and Havoc: Essays Into Human Learning and Education.* Portsmouth, NH: Heinemann.

Springer, L., Stanne, M. E., and Donovan, S. S. 1999. Effects of small-group learning on undergraduates in science, mathematics, engineering, and technology: A meta-analysis. *Review of Educational Research* 69, no. 1: 21–51.

Stanovich, K. E. 1986. Matthew effects in reading: Some consequences of individual differences in the acquisition of literacy. *Reading Research Quarterly* 21, no. 4: 360–407.

Sternberg, R. J. 1986. *Intelligence Applied: Understanding and Increasing Your Intellectual Skills.* San Diego, CA: Harcourt Brace Jovanovich.

Sternberg, R. J. 1996. *Successful Intelligence: How Practical and Creative Intelligence Determines Success in Life*. New York: Simon & Schuster.

Stiggins, R. 2002. Assessment crisis: The absence of assessment for learning. *Phi Delta Kappan* 83, no. 10: 758–765.

Stiggins, R. 2007. *Introduction to Student-Involved Classroom Assessment*, 5th Edition. Columbus, OH: Pearson Prentice Hall.

Sylwester, R. 1995. *A Celebration of Neurons: An Educator's Guide to the Brain*. Alexandria, VA: Association for Supervision and Curriculum Development.

Tieso, C. L. 2003. Ability grouping is not just tracking anymore. *Roeper Review* 26: 29–36.

Tjosvold, D. 1977. Alternate organizations for schools and classrooms. In D. Bartel and L. Saxe (Eds.), *Social Psychology of Education: Research and Theory*. New York: Hemisphere Press.

Tjosvold, D. and Santamaria, P. 1977. *The Effects of Cooperation and Teacher Support on Student Attitudes Toward Classroom Decision-Making*. Paper presented at the meeting of the American Educational Research Association, New York, March 1977.

Tomlinson, C. 1999. *The Differentiated Classroom: Responding to the Needs of All Learners*. Alexandria, VA: Association for Supervision and Curriculum Development.

Trumbull, E., Rothstein-Fisch, C., Greenfield, P. M., and Quiroz, B. 2001. *Bridging Cultures Between Home and School*. Mahwah, NJ: Erlbaum.

Tschannen-Moran, M. and Tschannen-Moran, B. 2010. *Evocative Coaching: Transforming Schools One Conversation at a Time*. San Francisco: Jossey-Bass.

von Frank, V. (Ed). 2007. *Finding Time for Professional Learning*. Oxford, OH: Learning Forward (formerly National Staff Development Council).

Vygotsky, L. S. 1962. *Thought and Language*. Cambridge, MA: Massachusetts Institute of Technology Press.

Vygotsky, L. S. 1978. *Mind and Society: The Development of Higher Psychological Processes*. Cambridge, MA: Harvard University Press.

Walters, J., Seidel, S., and Gardner, H. 1994. Children as reflective practitioners. In K. C. Block and J. N. Magnieri (Eds.), *Creating Powerful Thinking in Teachers and Students*. New York: Harcourt Brace.

Wasserman, S. G. and Ivany, J. W. 1988. *Teaching Elementary Science: Who's Afraid of Spiders?* New York: Harper & Row.

Wenger, E. 1998. *Communities of Practice: Learning, Meaning, and Identity*. Cambridge, MA: Cambridge University Press.

Wheatley, M. 2006. *Leadership and the New Science: Discovering Order in a Chaotic World*, 3rd Edition. San Francisco: Berrett-Kohler.

White, B. Y. and Frederiksen, J. R. 1998. Inquiry, modeling and meta-cognition: Making science accessible to all students. *Cognition and Instruction* 16, no. 1: 3–118.

Wiggins, G. 1993. *Assessing Student Performance: Exploring the Purpose and Limits of Testing*. San Francisco: Jossey-Bass.

Wiggins, G. and McTighe, J. 2005. *Understanding by Design*, 2nd Edition. Alexandria, VA: Association for Supervision and Curriculum Development.

Wolf, D. 1987. Opening up assessment. *Educational Leadership* 44, no. 4: 24–29.

Wolf, D. 1989. Portfolio assessment: Sampling student work. *Educational Leadership* 46, no. 7: 35–39.

Zessoules, R. and Gardner, H. 1991. Authentic assessment: Beyond the buzzword and into the classroom. In V. Perrone (Ed.), *Expanding Student Assessment* (pp. 47–71). Alexandria, VA: Association for Supervision and Curriculum Development.

Appendix 1: Standing on the Shoulders of Giants

" *If I have seen farther than others, it is because I was standing on the shoulders of giants.* "

Isaac Newton

We are often asked who to read and what to read. In this section, we briefly list the people and organizations whose thinking, writing, and actions have informed our work and who we think might help you deepen your own work as a leader. This is just a starting point. The greater the volume and scope of our reading, the more likely we are to learn and to support the learning of others and the organizations in which we work.

ASSESSMENT REFORM GROUP—including researchers such as Paul Black, Ruth Deakin Crick, John Gardner, Wynne Harlen, Mary James, and Gordon Stobart—has conducted several meta-analyses focused on classroom assessment that guide assessment-related decisions.

ROLAND BARTH (2004) is the founding director of Harvard University's Principals' Center and author of several books. His work centers around educational reform and school culture. He claims that leaders need to be active learners and they must create a culture of rich teacher leadership that values and celebrates the craft knowledge of the practitioner.

DAVID C. BERLINER and BRUCE J. BIDDLE (1997) in *The Manufactured Crisis* argue that the American school system is not really as inadequate as reported by the media and other government and industry sources. The book admits the existence of problems in the educational system, but insists that many of the charges levied against the schools are not true and that those charges fail to address the real dilemmas that American educators face.

SHIRLEY BRICE HEATH'S (1983) research study, *Ways with Words*, is a classic. Using children's language development, she showed the deep cultural differences between white and black working class communities and raised fundamental questions about the nature of language development, the effects of literacy on oral language habits, and the sources of communication problems in schools and workplaces.

JEROME BRUNER (1960, 1966, 1978, 1986, 1996) viewed cognitive dissonance as the key to learning. This is where discovery involves a reorganization of one's existing "truth" in order to account for new ideas. In *The Process of Education, Toward a Theory of Instruction* and *The Culture of Education,* he developed these arguments with respect to schooling (and education, more generally).

RUTH BUTLER'S research (1987, 1988) examines the role of feedback in learning. The research project compared marks only, comments only, and marks and comments combined. The group given comments only showed significantly greater learning gains.

WILFRED CARR and STEPHEN KEMMIS (1986) have helped educators come to appreciate action research as inquiry, whereby they use self-reflection in social situations in order to improve their own practice, their understanding of their practice, and the context in which they work. This research builds upon earlier work by KURT LEWIN.

MARIE CLAY (1993) was one of the first researchers in the field of literacy to examine and research what children—not adults—did as they read. The author of numerous research studies and programs, she is perhaps best known for her teacher's guidebook, *Reading Recovery: A Guidebook for Teachers in Training*.

ART COSTA and ROBERT GARMSTON (1994) developed cognitive coaching in 1984. They define it as a set of strategies and a way of thinking and working that support people to become more self-managing, self-monitoring, and self-modifying. Cognitive coaches assist colleagues to construct their own meaning through reflection and interaction.

MARTIN COVINGTON'S (1998) research and writing have been largely focused on understanding the motivational dynamics of school achievement. He has examined the interaction between students' social and academic goals and prevailing classroom reward structures.

TERENCE CROOKS (1998) researches and writes about educational assessment and the interrelationships among assessment, teaching, and learning. In 1988, he summarized ten years of classroom assessment research in a study titled, "The Impact of Classroom Evaluation Practices on Students."

LINDA DARLING-HAMMOND'S research includes teacher education, school leadership development, school redesign, educational equity, instruction of diverse learners, and education policy. Her research helps educators learn and transform their practice in a variety of educational arenas including work with students in classrooms.

TERRENCE DEAL and LEE BOLMAN (2008) have co-authored a number of books on leadership and organizations. They argue that effective leadership resides in the soul, faith, and powerful habits of mind. Further, when we examine our work from different perspectives or frames, we are more able to find powerful solutions.

EDWARD DECI and RICHARD RYAN (1985, 2002) have researched and written extensively about self-motivation, self-determination, self-regulation, and learning. Of particular interest is their work related to the use of rewards and the negative impact it has on learning and motivation.

LISA DELPIT (1995) analyzes the debate over meeting the educational needs of African-American and poor students. She concludes that all students must be taught the rules of power as a first step to a more just society. Further, teachers must acknowledge and validate minority students' home language.

JOHN DEWEY (1910) defined reflective thought as "active, persistent, and careful consideration of any belief or supposed form of knowledge in the light of the grounds that support it and the further conclusions to which it tends" (p. 6). His work contributed significantly to the evolution of education in North America.

SANFORD DORNBUSCH (1994) and JEANNIE OAKES (1985), working separately, have collected a significant body of research and writing to show the degree to which tracking in high schools limits student success and future opportunities.

RICHARD DUFOUR, REBECCA DUFOUR, and ROBERT EAKER have written extensively about the conceptual framework of professional learning communities. According to these authors, high-performing collaborative teams are built upon the essential blocks of mission, vision, values, and goals.

CAROL DWECK'S (2000) research examines the self-conceptions people use to structure the self and guide behavior, as well as their role in motivation, self-regulation, interpersonal processes, and achievement. One publication in particular, called *Self-Theories,* is a must-read for educators and parents.

JOYCE EPSTEIN (2010), director of the Center on School, Family, and Community Partnerships and the National Network of Partnership Schools, researches and writes about involving the community, school, and family in partnerships. Her framework for action teams centers around helping all students succeed in school and in later life.

REUVEN FEUERSTEIN (1990) viewed intelligence as an open, dynamic system that develops throughout life. He designed interventions called the "mediated learning experience" that enable children to make sense of the world around them.

MICHAEL FULLAN (2001), an internationally recognized authority on education reform, is engaged in training, consulting, and the evaluation of system-level change projects. He has written extensively about managing and driving educational change, focusing on building leadership capacity, on supporting effective change, and on promoting deep learning.

STEPHEN JAY GOULD (1981) wrote *The Mismeasure of Man*, a fascinating account of the history of psychometrics and intelligence testing. He encourages readers to rethink their assumptions and what they may consider as "truths" concerning intelligence and intelligence testing.

ANDY HARGREAVES (2003) has written many books and articles that center around change, culture, and leadership in education. His seven principles for sustainable leadership examine how educational innovation can promote deep and broad learning.

JOHN HATTIE (1992) researches and writes about how teachers can make a difference for student learning. Of particular interest is his work in the area of feedback and retention. He has tracked the research related to feedback over a number of years. His findings help us move forward in this critical area.

C. THOMAS HOLMES (1989) examined 63 empirical studies and found that retention harmed students' achievement, attendance record, personal adjustment in school, and attitude toward school.

ELLEN LANGER (1997) researches and writes about mindfulness in a variety of contexts. Her research in school settings causes one to rethink tried-and-true instructional methods and to consider classroom assessment.

LEARNING FORWARD (formerly the NATIONAL STAFF DEVELOPMENT COUNCIL) is a non-profit professional association that focuses on providing leadership, information, and research regarding effective professional development. Learning Forward has created standards indicating that staff development must be results-driven, standards-based, and job-embedded.

PAUL LEMAHIEU (1996), currently senior partner for design, development, and research at the Carnegie Foundation for the Advancement of Teaching, and University of Hawaii, Manoa, has researched and written extensively about portfolios and accounting for learning. His work has helped us to see how portfolios can be productively used for large-scale assessment, as well as to inform classroom assessment.

ROBERT MARZANO (2000) is cofounder and CEO of Marzano Research Laboratory and has researched and written extensively about classroom and school leadership, and how leadership behaviors impact student achievement.

NORMA MICKELSON's research and teaching enriched the field of children's verbal learning and literacy evaluation. She was a pioneer in contextualized literacy learning.

MARIA MONTESSORI (1870–1952) was the first woman in Italy to qualify as a physician. The education program she developed focused on first educating the senses and then the intellect. The success of her method caused her to ask questions of "normal" education and the ways in which it failed children.

ANTOINETTE OBERG's research and teaching in curriculum studies have influenced many educators. Her ability to listen deeply and help other researchers find their way to truth is well documented. The research methods her work employs provide a model for others seeking to inquire more mindfully.

TOM PETERS and BOB WATERMAN's (1982) leadership wisdom was first published in *In Search of Excellence*. Since then they have continued to encourage leaders to take action, to build relationships, and to acquire and grow the best employees. Their ideas have guided both business and education.

JAMES PROCHASKA, JOHN NORCROSS, and CARLO DICLEMENTE (1994), authors of *Changing for Good: A Revolutionary Six-Stage Program for Overcoming Bad Habits and Moving Your Life Positively Forward* (1994), amassed almost three decades of research examining how habits are changed. Consciously moving through the stages they outline improves your chances of changing your habit. This work is useful when considering the habits of educators with regard to teaching, assessing, and evaluating others.

DOUGLAS REEVES (2007) is the founder of The Leadership and Learning Center, a professional development and consulting services division of Houghton Mifflin Harcourt, a leading global education organization. His work in the area of assessment has been both practical and accessible to educators.

ROBERT ROSENTHAL and LENORE JACOBSON (1992) published *Pygmalion in the Classroom: Teacher Expectation and Pupils' Intellectual Development* in 1968. This book argues that student behavior is influenced by teacher expectations—that is, when teachers expect students to do well, they tend to do well; when teachers expect students to fail, they tend to fail.

ROYCE SADLER'S (1989) work focuses on assessing student learning, grading, assessment policy and practice, and improving university teaching. His article "Formative Assessment and the Design of Instructional Systems" articulates the reasons why clear criteria are necessary if students are to learn and serves as a foundation for subsequent work in formative assessment.

PHILLIP SCHLECHTY (2009) is the founder and CEO of the Center for Leadership in School Reform (CLSR) and author of numerous books on school reform, including *Leading for Learning: How to Transform Schools Into Learning Organizations, Shaking Up the Schoolhouse, Schools for the 21st Century, Inventing Better Schools*, and *Working on the Work*. The key to improving education, argues Schlechty, lies in providing better quality work for students—work that is engaging and that enables students to learn what they need in order to succeed.

DONALD SCHÖN'S (1983, 1987) early work focused on learning systems within organizations and communities. He was one of the first thinkers to conceptualize learning organizations where "feedback loops" inform the system. His later work explored reflective practice: reflection-in-action and reflection-on-action.

PETER SENGE (2006) writes about innovative learning organizations in terms of systems thinking, personal mastery, mental models, shared vision, and team learning. From an assessment perspective, his work is particularly important because of the reliance on continuous reflective feedback.

THOMAS J. SERGIOVANNI (1994) is an internationally recognized author on educational leadership. His work has helped schools and systems rethink how they can operate successfully. His five dimensions of leadership—technical, human, educational, cultural, and symbolic—are lenses through which effective leadership practice can be strengthened.

LORRIE A. SHEPARD'S (1989, 2000) research focus includes evaluating test use, grade retention, teacher testing, effects of high-stakes testing, and classroom assessment. Her research studies on the effects of retention and its relationship to the dropout rate found that students who repeated were 20 to 30 percent more likely to drop out of school.

ROBERT STERNBERG (1986, 1996) views intelligence as modifiable rather than fixed. Research suggests that successful intelligent people achieve success by identifying and capitalizing on their strengths, and identifying and correcting or compensating for their weaknesses. His theory is called "practical intelligence."

RICK STIGGINS (2007) has focused most of his career in helping educators become more assessment-literate. He writes: "If we wish to maximize student achievement in the U.S., we must pay far greater attention to the improvement of classroom assessment. Both assessment *of* learning and assessment *for* learning are essential" (Stiggins 2002, p. 765). Stiggins stresses the importance of building student confidence in order to maximize learning and achievement.

LEV VYGOTSKY (1962, 1978) viewed the individual's development through social interactions with others. He coined the term *zone of proximal development*. Vygotsky considered language as the primary tool of intellectual transformation. His theories continue to support further exploration into learning theory.

BRUCE WELLMAN and ROBERT GARMSTON (2009) write about developing collaborative groups and effective professional development. Their work in adaptive schools provides school staffs with resources and strategies to create collaborative norms, to design and conduct effective meetings, to engage in learning-focused conversations, and to become skilled at group facilitation.

ETIENNE WENGER (1998) and JEAN LAVE coined the term *community of practice*. A growing number of people and organizations, including educators such as Richard DuFour, are using the idea of communities of practice as a key to supporting learning and improving performance. Etienne Wenger's book *Communities of Practice* is a very helpful resource for educational leaders.

MARGARET WHEATLEY (2006) is co-founder and president emeritus of the Berkana Institute. Her work centers around having the courage to reclaim conversation and applying the lens of "living systems theory" to organizations and communities.

B. Y. WHITE and J. R. FREDERIKSEN (1998) carried out a study in California with 12 science classes in two schools, involving children aged 12 and 13. It focused on self- and peer assessment; the outcome was not only better learning, but also gains for the students at the lower end.

Appendix 2:
Reproducibles

The following reproducibles are provided for leaders to adapt to their own use, ensuring that the credits and copyright information appear on every page that is copied.

To enlarge to 8½ x 11 inches, please set photocopier at 115%.

Communication Planning Tool

Overall Message:

Top Three Talking Points	Visual Representation
Possible Audiences	Possible Methods	Possible Opportunities

Reference page 12 in text.

Review Checklist

The policy reflects these principles of assessment *for* learning	Met	On the Way	Beginning	Not Yet Met
Supports and reflects curricular outcomes and standards				
Engages students in the learning process as partners				
Focuses on "what" and "how" students learn				
Recognizes all educational achievement, not just academic				
Honors assessment as an ongoing, systematic process				
Involves parents				
Requires assessment to be balanced and multifaceted				
Respects the dignity and reflects the developmental needs of the learner				
Is equitable and fair				
Recognizes assessment as a key professional skill				

Reference page 27 in text.

System Change Using Assessment *for* Learning

School leadership teams composed of the school principal and faculty meet for one day together two or three times during each school year. The purpose is to learn about change, about assessment *for* learning at the district, school, adult learner, and student levels, and consider ways to transform emerging barriers. During the last gathering, teams meet to show proof of learning.

At the same time, the district leadership undertakes a transparent process of reviewing policies, regulations, and practices such as assessment, evaluation, reporting, and communicating evidence of learning at all levels.

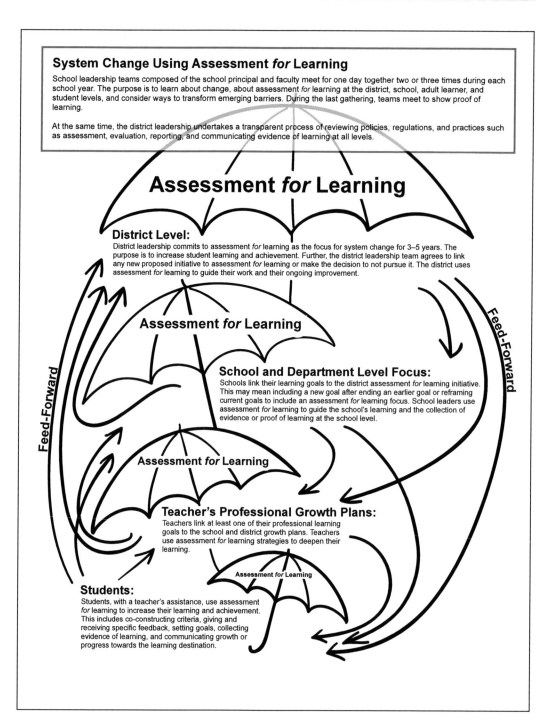

Assessment *for* Learning

District Level:
District leadership commits to assessment *for* learning as the focus for system change for 3–5 years. The purpose is to increase student learning and achievement. Further, the district leadership team agrees to link any new proposed initiative to assessment *for* learning or make the decision to not pursue it. The district uses assessment *for* learning to guide their work and their ongoing improvement.

Assessment *for* Learning

School and Department Level Focus:
Schools link their learning goals to the district assessment *for* learning initiative. This may mean including a new goal after ending an earlier goal or reframing current goals to include an assessment *for* learning focus. School leaders use assessment *for* learning to guide the school's learning and the collection of evidence or proof of learning at the school level.

Assessment *for* Learning

Teacher's Professional Growth Plans:
Teachers link at least one of their professional learning goals to the school and district growth plans. Teachers use assessment *for* learning strategies to deepen their learning.

Assessment *for* Learning

Students:
Students, with a teacher's assistance, use assessment *for* learning to increase their learning and achievement. This includes co-constructing criteria, giving and receiving specific feedback, setting goals, collecting evidence of learning, and communicating growth or progress towards the learning destination.

Feed-Forward

Feed-Forward

Reference page 28 in text.

Reflecting Frame

Recollection	
Application	
Insight	

Reference page 32 in text.

Don't Do List

Reference page 44 in text.

Teacher:
Area of Focus:
Connection to School Plan:

STEP ONE

ACTION AREA	WHAT AM I GOING TO DO?	WHAT PROFESSIONAL SUPPORT IS REQUIRED?	WHAT DOES THE BASELINE STUDENT EVIDENCE TELL ME?
Specify current level of student performance.			

STEP TWO

ACTION AREA	WHAT AM I GOING TO DO?	WHAT PROFESSIONAL SUPPORT IS REQUIRED?	WHAT DOES THE STUDENT EVIDENCE TELL ME?
Create an action plan: • Specify a measurable, instructional goal. • Describe teaching practice. • Describe assessment practice with time lines.			

STEP THREE

ACTION AREA	WHAT AM I GOING TO DO?	WHAT PROFESSIONAL SUPPORT IS REQUIRED?	WHAT DOES THE STUDENT EVIDENCE TELL ME?
Evaluate progress.			

Reference page 48 in text.

Professional Learning Structure	Who is participating?	What is the purpose?	When will it take place?	How will it take place?
Example:				

Reference page 53 in text.

Using the frame, what activities and/or questions could your leadership team use as you move through the phases of learning?

Phase	Questions
Activate	
Acquire	
Apply	

Reference page 54 in text.

Professional Growth Plan

Name:
Position:
School:

Outcomes:

Connection to School, District, or State Plans:

Strategies:

Expected Student Outcomes:

Evidence of Success:

Reference page 58 in text.

Assessment Plan for:
Grade Level:

Destination	Evidence of Learning
What does it look like and sound like to be successful at the end of the year?	What evidence will the learner have? How can the learner show his/her learning to others?
Samples / Models	**Evaluation**
What samples, exemplars, or anchors do you have that show quality? (They need to reflect a range.) For what evidence do you need to involve the learner in setting the criteria?	How will you know you are successful? What evidence will your professional judgment be based on?

Reference page 67 in text.

Working Through Resistance

• What is happening? What is the situation? What is going on here?

• What is my/our personal reaction to this?

• Why do I/we think that this is happening?

• What may be some consequences if this continues?

• What am I/are we willing to do about it? What will my/our initial response be?

• How can I/we manage my/our personal reaction?

Reference page 75 in text.

The Seven Norms of Collaborative Work

Pausing: Pausing before responding or asking a question allows time for thinking and enhances dialogue, discussion, and decision making.

Paraphrasing: Using paraphrase helps members of the group to hear and understand each other as they formulate decisions.

Probing: Using gentle open-ended probes or inquiries such as, "Please say more about . . ." or "I'm curious about . . ." increases the clarity and precision of the group's thinking.

Putting ideas on the table: Ideas are the heart of a meaningful dialogue.

Paying attention to self and others: Meaningful dialogue is facilitated when each group member is conscious of self and of others, and is aware of not only what she/he is saying, but also how it is said and how others are responding.

Presuming positive intentions: Assuming that others' intentions are positive promotes and facilitates meaningful dialogue and eliminates unintentional put-downs.

Pursuing a balance between advocacy and inquiry: Pursuing and maintaining a balance between advocating a position and inquiring about one's own and others' positions help the group to become a learning organization.

Adapted from *The Adaptive School: Developing and Facilitating Collaborative Groups* by Robert Garmston and Bruce Wellman. Used with permission.

Reference page 89 in text.

Working With Parents and Community

Example	Providing information	Receiving information	Making decisions / setting direction together
Community member participates as part of a group of adults who assess student end-of-year exit interviews			
Student-parent-teacher conferences take place before report card is written			
Community action team			
Parents and students work together through a package of student work samples			
Parent focus groups provide feedback to policy development			
Parent representation on school planning committee			
Parent representation on school district committees			

Reference page 90 in text.

Plan for Using Data

Guiding Questions	Consider . . .	Your Notes
What is our goal/target? What data could we collect in order to provide proof of reaching the stated goal/target?	-Data from differentiated sources -Student assessment data that include a broad range of sources -School-based data -District-based data	
Who will collect the data?	-External support -Internal support	
When will the data be collected?	-Monthly -Three times per year -Once per year	
How will the data be collected?	-Electronically -District-generated forms -Sent in by each school	
Who will collate the data? How?	-Committee -Individual -External support -Internal support	
Who will analyze the data?	-Committee -Superintendent's department -Board of trustees	
How will the findings be reported?	-Formal report -Executive summary -Brochure	
To whom will the findings be reported?	-System personnel -Community -Selected group	
When will the findings be reported?	-Yearly -Twice a year -Quarterly	

Reference page 99 in text.

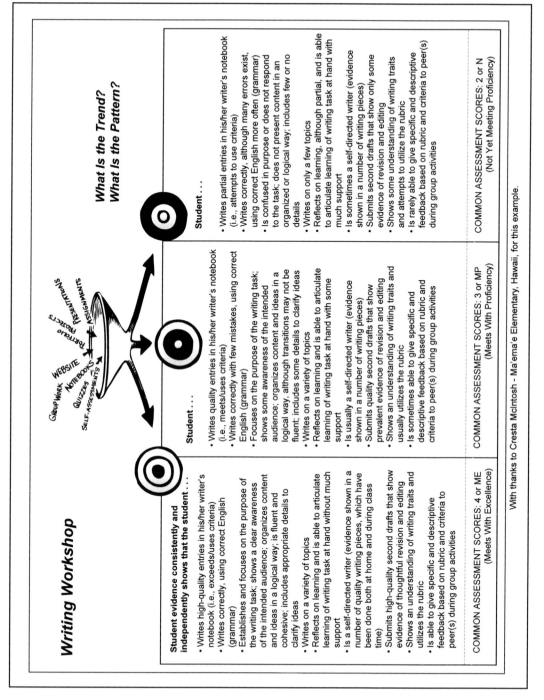

Writing Workshop

What Is the Trend?
What Is the Pattern?

Student evidence consistently and independently shows that the student . . .

- Writes high-quality entries in his/her writer's notebook (i.e., exceeds/uses criteria)
- Writes correctly, using correct English (grammar)
- Establishes and focuses on the purpose of the writing task; shows a clear awareness of the intended audience; organizes content and ideas in a logical way; is fluent and cohesive; includes appropriate details to clarify ideas
- Writes on a variety of topics
- Reflects on learning and is able to articulate learning of writing task at hand without much support
- Is a self-directed writer (evidence shown in a number of quality writing pieces, which have been done both at home and during class time)
- Submits high-quality second drafts that show evidence of thoughtful revision and editing
- Shows an understanding of writing traits and utilizes the rubric
- Is able to give specific and descriptive feedback based on rubric and criteria to peer(s) during group activities

COMMON ASSESSMENT SCORES: 4 or ME
(Meets With Excellence)

Student . . .

- Writes quality entries in his/her writer's notebook (i.e., meets/uses criteria)
- Writes correctly with few mistakes, using correct English (grammar)
- Focuses on the purpose of the writing task; shows some awareness of the intended audience; organizes content and ideas in a logical way, although transitions may not be fluent; includes some details to clarify ideas
- Writes on a variety of topics
- Reflects on learning and is able to articulate learning of writing task at hand with some support
- Is usually a self-directed writer (evidence shown in a number of writing pieces)
- Submits quality second drafts that show prevalent evidence of revision and editing
- Shows an understanding of writing traits and usually utilizes the rubric
- Is sometimes able to give specific and descriptive feedback based on rubric and criteria to peer(s) during group activities

COMMON ASSESSMENT SCORES: 3 or MP
(Meets With Proficiency)

Student . . .

- Writes partial entries in his/her writer's notebook (i.e., attempts to use criteria)
- Writes correctly, although many errors exist, using correct English more often (grammar)
- Is confused in purpose or does not respond to the task; does not present content in an organized or logical way; includes few or no details
- Writes on only a few topics
- Reflects on learning, although partial, and is able to articulate learning of writing task at hand with much support
- Is sometimes a self-directed writer (evidence shown in a number of writing pieces)
- Submits second drafts that show only some evidence of revision and editing
- Shows some understanding of writing traits and attempts to utilize the rubric
- Is rarely able to give specific and descriptive feedback based on rubric and criteria to peer(s) during group activities

COMMON ASSESSMENT SCORES: 2 or N
(Not Yet Meeting Proficiency)

With thanks to Cresta McIntosh - Ma'ema'e Elementary, Hawaii, for this example.

Reference page 107 in text.

Learning Destination for:	Possible Evidence	My Evidence Includes
As you look at my evidence, please notice . . .		

Adapted from *Conferencing and Reporting* by Gregory, Cameron, and Davies, 2011.

Reference page 110 in text.

Activity: Evaluation—Exploring Letter Grades

Arrange to have one or two plates with something good to eat wrapped tightly with clear plastic (e.g., candies, cookies, different squares) available for this activity. It is important to note that each plate needs to contain five different kinds of items and hold enough so everyone in the room can have at least one to eat when the activity is finished. For example, each plate contains two Tootsie Rolls, two mini chocolate bars, two packages of licorice, two individually wrapped toffees, and two mini Rice Krispie squares. Participants are asked to look but not touch.

This activity is done in three stages.

Step 1. Ask participants to make a judgment and give each kind of item a letter grade (A, B, C) without talking or without showing others what they have done. This is an individual activity only.

Step 2. When finished, ask participants to work with their group and, through discussion, come to agreement, and assign letter grades to each item. No voting or intimidation. Group members need to reach consensus after dialogue.

Step 3. When the groups are finished, ask them to number off and form into new groups and become a representative of their group. Their task is to come to agreement again around their previous evaluation in their new group.

Reference page 112 in text.

Anne Davies, Ph.D., is a researcher, writer, and educational consultant. She has also been a teacher, school administrator, and system leader. Anne has taught at universities both in Canada and the United States, including University of Victoria and University of Southern Maine. Anne is the author of more than 30 books and multi-media resources, as well as numerous chapters and articles. Since 2001, Anne has been a member of the team representing Canada at the International Conference on Assessment *for* Learning. It has been held in United Kingdom (2001), United States (2004), New Zealand (2009), and Norway (2011). A recipient of the Hilroy Fellowship for Innovative Teaching, Anne continues to support others to learn more about assessment in the service of learning and learners.

Sandra Herbst is a noted system leader, author, speaker, and consultant with over 20 years of experience. She has worked in both elementary and secondary schools and is a former classroom and specialty teacher, school administrator, program consultant, and assistant superintendent of a large urban district. Sandra is a past president of the Manitoba Association of School Superintendents and the Manitoba ASCD affiliate. She has facilitated professional learning in schools, districts, and organizations across North America in the areas of leadership, instruction, assessment, and evaluation. Her school and district experiences deeply connect learners to practical and possible strategies and approaches. She is the co-author of two books on the topic of assessment.

Beth Parrott Reynolds, Ph.D., is the president and performance consultant for Leadership for Learning, Inc. and a practicing school improvement specialist. She is a former English teacher, high school principal, and assistant superintendent with more than 30 years of experience in leading schools and districts to develop the internal capacity needed to drive change for student and organizational success. In addition to keynotes, Beth is often asked to lead deep work with schools and districts in areas including standards, assessment, instruction, and grading. She is the co-author of two books on the topic of assessment.